HOW TO USE THIS STUDY

Objectives

Most guides in the LIFECHANGE series of Bible studies cover one book of the Bible. Although the LIFECHANGE guides vary with the books they explore, they share some common goals:

1. To provide you with a firm foundation of understanding and a thirst to return to the book;
2. To teach you by example how to study a book of the Bible without structured guides;
3. To give you all the historical background, word definitions, and explanatory notes you need, so that your only other reference is the Bible;
4. To help you grasp the message of the book as a whole;
5. To teach you how to let God's Word transform you into Christ's image.

Each lesson in this study is designed to take 60 to 90 minutes to complete on your own. The guide is based on the assumption that you are completing one lesson per week, but if time is limited you can do half a lesson per week or whatever amount allows you to be thorough.

Flexibility

LIFECHANGE guides are flexible, allowing you to adjust the quantity and depth of your study to meet your individual needs. The guide offers many optional questions in addition to the regular numbered questions. The optional questions, which appear in the margins of the study pages, include the following:

Optional Application. Nearly all application questions are optional; we hope you will do as many as you can without overcommitting yourself.

For Thought and Discussion. Beginning Bible students should be able to handle these, but even advanced students need to think about them. These questions frequently deal with ethical issues and other biblical principles. They often offer cross-references to spark thought, but the references do not give obvious answers. They are good for group discussions.

5

For Further Study. These include: a) cross-references that shed light on a topic the book discusses, and b) questions that delve deeper into the passage. You can omit them to shorten a lesson without missing a major point of the passage.

If you are meeting in a group, decide together which optional questions to prepare for each lesson, and how much of the lesson you will cover at the next meeting. Normally, the group leader should make this decision, but you might let each member choose his or her own application questions.

As you grow in your walk with God, you will find the LIFECHANGE guide growing with you—a helpful reference on a topic, a continuing challenge for application, a source of questions for many levels of growth.

Overview and Details

The study begins with an overview of the book of Mark. The key to interpretation is context—what is the whole passage or book *about?*—and the key to context is purpose—what is the author's *aim* for the whole work? In lesson one you will lay the foundation for your study of Mark by asking yourself, "Why did the author (and God) write the book? What did they want to accomplish? What is the book about?"

In lessons two through eighteen you will analyze successive passages of Mark in detail.

After you have completed the final lesson, you may want to review Mark, returning to the big picture to see whether your view of it has changed after closer study. Review will also strengthen your grasp of major issues and give you an idea of how you have grown from your study.

Kinds of Questions

Bible study on your own—without a structured guide—follows a progression. First you observe: What does the passage *say?* Then you interpret: What does the passage *mean?* Lastly you apply: How does this truth *affect* my life?

Some of the "how" and "why" questions will take some creative thinking, even prayer, to answer. Some are opinion questions without clear-cut right answers; these will lend themselves to discussions and side studies.

Don't let your study become an exercise of knowledge alone. Treat the passage as God's Word, and stay in dialogue with Him as you study. Pray, "Lord, what do You want me to see here?" "Father, why is this true?" "Lord, how does this apply to my life?"

It is important that you write down your answers. The act of writing clarifies your thinking and helps you to remember.

Study Aids

A list of reference materials, including a few notes of explanation to help you make good use of them, begins on page 169.

This guide is designed to include enough background to let you interpret with

A NavPress Bible study on the book of

MARK

NAVPRESS

NAVPRESS⊘

NavPress is the publishing ministry of The Navigators, an international Christian organization and leader in personal spiritual development. NavPress is committed to helping people grow spiritually and enjoy lives of meaning and hope through personal and group resources that are biblically rooted, culturally relevant, and highly practical.

For a free catalog go to www.NavPress.com
or call 1.800.366.7788 in the United States or 1.800.839.4769 in Canada.

ISBN 978-0-89109-910-9

Unless otherwise identified, all Scripture quotations are from the *Holy Bible: New International Version* (NIV). Copyright © 1973, 1978, 1984, International Bible Society. Used by permission of Zondervan Bible Publishers. Other versions used are the *New American Standard Bible* (NASB), © The Lockman Foundation 1960, 1962, 1963, 1968, 1971, 1972, 1973, 1975, 1977; and the *King James Version* (KJV).

Printed in the United States of America

9 10 11 12 13 14 15 16 / 14 13 12 11 10 09

CONTENTS

ACKNOWLEDGMENTS

The LIFECHANGE series has been produced through the coordinated efforts of a team of Navigator Bible study developers and NavPress editorial staff, along with a nationwide network of fieldtesters.

AUTHOR: TED DORMAN
SERIES EDITOR: KAREN LEE-THORP

just your Bible and the guide. Still, if you want more information on a subject or want to study a book on your own, try the references listed.

Scripture Versions

Unless otherwise indicated, the Bible quotations in this guide are from the New International Version of the Bible. Other versions cited are the New American Standard Bible (NASB) and the King James Version (KJV).

Use any translation you like for study, preferably more than one. A paraphrase such as The Living Bible is not accurate enough for study, but it can be helpful for comparison or devotional reading.

Memorizing and Meditating

A psalmist wrote, "I have hidden your word in my heart that I might not sin against you" (Psalm 119:11). If you write down a verse or passage that challenges or encourages you, and reflect on it often for a week or more, you will find it beginning to affect your motives and actions. We forget quickly what we read once; we remember what we ponder.

When you find a significant verse or passage, you might copy it onto a card to keep with you. Set aside five minutes during each day just to think about what the passage might mean in your life. Recite it over to yourself, exploring its meaning. Then, return to your passage as often as you can during your day, for a brief review. You will soon find it coming to mind spontaneously.

For Group Study

A group of four to ten people allows the richest discussions, but you can adapt this guide for other sized groups. It will suit a wide range of group types, such as home Bible studies, growth groups, youth groups, and businessmen's studies. Both new and experienced Bible students, and new and mature Christians, will benefit from the guide. You can omit or leave for later years any questions you find too easy or too hard.

The guide is intended to lead a group through one lesson per week. However, feel free to split lessons if you want to discuss them more thoroughly. Or, omit some questions in a lesson if preparation or discussion time is limited. You can always return to this guide for personal study later. You will be able to discuss only a few questions at length, so choose some for discussion and others for background. Make time at each discussion for members to ask about anything they didn't understand.

Each lesson in the guide ends with a section called "For the group." These sections give advice on how to focus a discussion, how you might apply the lesson in your group, how you might shorten a lesson, and so on. The group leader should read each "For the group" at least a week ahead so that he or she can tell the group how to prepare for the next lesson.

Each member should prepare for a meeting by writing answers for all of the background and discussion questions to be covered. If the group decides not to take an hour per week for private preparation, then expect to take at least two meetings per lesson to work through the questions. Application will be very difficult, however, without private thought and prayer.

Two reasons for studying in a group are accountability and support. When each member commits in front of the rest to seek growth in an area of life, you can pray with one another, listen jointly for God's guidance, help one another to resist temptation, assure each other that the other's growth matters to you, use the group to practice spiritual principles, and so on. Pray about one another's commitments and needs at most meetings. Spend the first few minutes of each meeting sharing any results from applications prompted by previous lessons. Then discuss new applications toward the end of the meeting. Follow such sharing with prayer for these and other needs.

If you write down each other's applications and prayer requests, you are more likely to remember to pray for them during the week, ask about them at the next meeting, and notice answered prayers. You might want to get a notebook for prayer requests and discussion notes.

Notes taken during discussion will help you to remember, follow up on ideas, stay on the subject, and clarify a total view of an issue. But don't let note-taking keep keep you from participating. Some groups choose one member at each meeting to take notes. Then someone copies the notes and distributes them at the next meeting. Rotating these tasks can help include people. Some groups have someone take notes on a large pad of paper or erasable marker board (preformed shower wallboard works well), so that everyone can see what has been recorded.

Pages 171-172 list some good sources of counsel for leading group studies.

Key Places in the Book of Mark

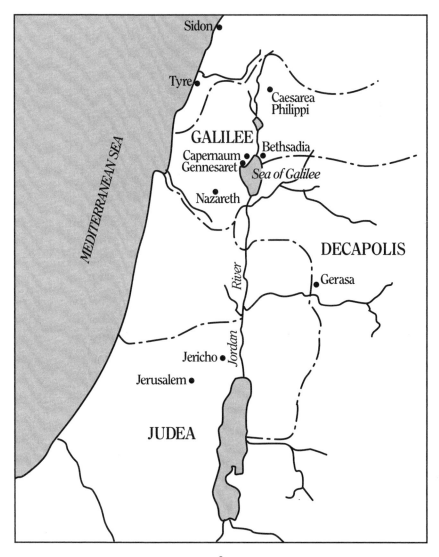

BACKGROUND

Mark and His Gospel

Who was Mark?

Tradition ascribes the Gospel of Mark to a first-century Jewish Christian named John Mark. That is, John was his first name, and Mark (or Marcus) was his surname. His Latin surname may indicate that he, like the Apostle Paul, was a Roman citizen. His mother was a Christian woman named Mary, who lived in Jerusalem and was well-acquainted with the Apostle Peter (Acts 12:12). John Mark was also cousin to Barnabas, Paul's earliest missionary companion (Colossians 4:10).

We do not know whether the author of this Gospel was an eyewitness to the ministry of Jesus. If John Mark was indeed the author, he would have had opportunity as a resident of Jerusalem to see Jesus. But whether or not he was in fact an eyewitness (as some believe Mark 14:51-52 implies), his connections with Peter (1 Peter 5:13), Paul, and Barnabas gave him a firsthand knowledge of the apostolic traditions about Jesus. Indeed, the second-century church historians Papias and Irenaeus wrote that Mark's Gospel was basically a record of the preaching material of Peter. More recently, the late T. W. Manson theorized that Mark was Peter's interpreter or aide-de-camp during Peter's ministry in Rome.[1]

While the Gospel of Mark does not identify its author, John Mark's background and training, combined with the early Church tradition, which names this Gospel after him, make it likely that the man whom Peter called "my son" was indeed the author of the shortest of our four gospel accounts.

Date and audience

Modern scholars are virtually unanimous in viewing Mark as the earliest of the four Gospels. Many historians believe Mark wrote his gospel account after the death of Peter but before the fall of Jerusalem—i.e., between AD 64 and 70.

The text of Mark's Gospel makes it virtually certain that he was writing to a Gentile audience. For example, the fact that Mark explains certain Jewish practices to his readers means that they must have been unfamiliar with them (7:3-4,

15:42). In addition, Aramaic forms that remain in the text are interpreted (5:41, 7:34, 14:36).

While it is less certain where Mark wrote his Gospel, Rome seems the most attractive alternative (see, for example, the note on Mark 12:42, as well as other notes throughout the study guide). Other suggested venues include Egypt and Syria.

Purpose

Mark seeks to explain to Gentiles, whether Christians or nonChristians inquiring about Jesus, how the Jewish Messiah was rejected by His own people because He came in a way they did not expect: not as a glorious warrior-king, but as a suffering servant. In this way Mark grounds the gospel message in history, so that his readers might know (1) that the message they have heard is true, despite its being rejected by the Jewish nation, and (2) that the gospel is the fulfillment of God's promises through and to Israel, and cannot be understood apart from that historical context. Mark's emphasis on suffering and persecution may also be relevant to his readers' situation if they were Roman Christians during Nero's persecution (about AD 65).

Mark's relationship to Matthew and Luke

Gospel is an Old English word that means "good news." It translates the Greek word *euangelion* (*eu-,* "good" and *angelion*, "message"), which also gives us words like "evangelist" and is related to words like "angel."

When the first Christians wanted to record the "good news" about the Man who was God, none of the familiar forms of literature seemed suitable. The Christians didn't write the kinds of biographies or sacred texts that were common in Greek, Roman, or Jewish culture. Instead, they created a new form: the Gospel.

One need not be a scholar to recognize the strong resemblance between the Gospel of Mark and those of Matthew and Luke. John's Gospel, while preserving a few of the traditions present in the other three, is written from a much different perspective. Hence Mark, Matthew, and Luke are called the *synoptic* Gospels (from the Greek word meaning "to see together").

Because Mark is much shorter than either Matthew or Luke, Christian writers from the second century onward tended to neglect it in favor of its lengthier counterparts. Matthew's Gospel was generally the most popular; Saint Augustine, for example, believed that Matthew was written first, with Mark being a sort of *Reader's Digest* condensed version.

Within the last two hundred years biblical scholars have generally argued that Mark is the earliest of the four gospel accounts. Among the points of evidence they cite are the following:

- Mark may be divided into 105 sections. Of these, ninety-three occur in Matthew and eighty-one in Luke.
- Mark contains 661 verses, compared to Matthew's 1,068 and Luke's 1,149. Of these 661 verses in Mark, Matthew includes 606 (with some variation), while

Luke includes 320. Only thirty-one of Mark's verses do not occur in either Matthew or Luke.

■ Matthew occasionally varies Mark's order of events. So does Luke. Matthew and Luke together, however, *never* vary Mark's order. One of them always agrees with Mark's order of events; most often, both do.

■ Matthew and Luke frequently "smooths the rough edges" off Mark's rather coarse Greek. Matthew tends to simplify the language of the Markan accounts he uses, while Luke often improves them stylistically. At other times, however, Matthew and Luke—particularly Matthew—reproduce Mark's language exactly.

On the basis of these considerations, among others, it is reasonable to believe that both Matthew and Luke had at least portions of Mark's Gospel at their disposal when they wrote their own. A few modern scholars hold out for Matthew's being the earliest written Gospel account, but this view is not generally accepted. Thus it appears that John Mark, cousin of Barnabas and companion to both Peter and Paul, was the creator of the Gospel format.

1. T. W. Manson, "The Foundation of the Synoptic Tradition," *Bulletin of the John Rylands Library* xxviii (1944), pages 132-133. Cited by F. F. Bruce, *Commentary on the Epistles to the Ephesians and Colossians* (Grand Rapids, MI: William B. Eerdmans Publishing Co., 1957), page 305. See also the Rev. Msgr. Michael J. Wrenn's article in *Fidelity* (November 1987, pages 8-13), which contends that Mark's Gospel is a Greek translation of Peter's account of Jesus' life, death, and resurrection, written originally in Hebrew.

OVERVIEW

Mark

Before beginning an in-depth study of Mark's Gospel, one should get a general overview of the book by reading it straight through. This should not take much more than one hour, provided that you do not spend too much time pondering difficult passages (save that for a later reading!). Your first reading should be a time to gain first impressions, as though you were reading a novel.

As you read, consider the following:

First impressions

1. The very first words a person says often give us a clue as to what he or she will be talking about.

   a. What are Mark's first words (1:1)? What do they tell us about his Gospel?

   _____

   _____

   _____

   b. What are the first words of Jesus (1:15)? What is the main theme of His preaching?

   _____

   _____

   _____

For Thought and
Discussion: What
new insights have you
received from your initial
reading of Mark?

Optional Application:
Choose one of the key
ideas you found while
reading through Mark,
and pray that God will
give you wisdom as to
how you might apply it
to your life in the weeks
to come.

2. Repetition of key words or phrases is also a clue to
finding out what the author is trying to communicate. As you read through Mark's Gospel, jot down:

a. The references where he repeats the key words
and phrases referred to in question 1.

_____

_____

_____

_____

_____

_____

b. Other words or phrases you see as being key
terms. (Do not take too long to do this during the
first reading; you can come back and add to your
list as you proceed through the study guide.)

_____

_____

_____

_____

_____

_____

3. Perhaps the most important element of interpretation is discerning the flow of the author's thought.
The chapter and verse divisions in our Bibles were
created long after the books were written and are
sometimes even obstacles to following the author's
train of thought. Don't read the Gospel of Mark as a
collection of proof-texts to be repeated in isolation
from one another. Rather, read Mark as you would
any other book: a story consisting of sentences and
paragraphs which relate to one another.

1:1 Title

1:2-13　　　　　　　Preparing the way

1:14–10:52　　　　　　Jesus and the Kingdom of God

   1:14–4:34 _____

     1:14-15 _____

     1:16-45 _____

     2:1–3:6 _____

     3:7-35_____

     4:1-34_____

   4:35–9:29 _____

     4:35–5:43 _____

     6:1-6 _____

     6:7-13_____

     6:14-29 _____

     6:30-56 _____

     7:1-23_____

     7:24–8:10 _____

     8:11-21 _____

     8:22-26 _____

     8:27–9:13 _____

     9:14-29 _____

   9:30–10:52_____

     9:30-50 _____

     10:1-12 _____

     10:13-31_____

     10:32-45_____

     10:46-52_____

Optional Application:
If the life and ministry of Jesus are indeed only the "beginning" of the Gospel, what implications does this have that apply to you?

11:1–16:20 _____

The Final Week

11:1-11 _____

11:12-26 _____

11:27–12:44 _____

13:1-37 _____

14:1-42 _____

14:43–15:15 _____

15:16-47 _____

16:1-8 _____

16:9-20 _____

The beginning of the Gospel (Mark 1:1)

Christ (1:1). From the Greek *christos,* "anointed one." A translation of the Hebrew *mashiach,* "Messiah." In the Old Testament, kings of Israel were anointed with oil as a sign of their spiritual authority, with the oil representing the Spirit of God. See, for example, 1 Samuel 16:13.

Son of God (1:1). In the Old Testament this title usually refers to the people of Israel or the king of Israel. Thus the ideas of being chosen (as were God's people) and of deserving obedience (as the king did) are present. The title "Son of God" does not refer to the coming Messiah in the Old Testament, but was probably just coming into use as a messianic title when Jesus arrived on the scene.

---

4. Mark 1:1 is either an introduction to verses 2-8, or a title for the entire Gospel of Mark.

    a. Compare Mark 1:1 with Acts 1:1. Does this help you decide whether the word "beginning" refers to John the Baptist (1:2-8), or to the life and ministry of Jesus (the entire Gospel of Mark)? If so, why?

18

_____

_____

_____

b. If the word "beginning" is a title for the entire book, what does this tell us about the "gospel about Jesus Christ"?

_____

_____

_____

For the group

This "For the group" section and the ones in later lessons are intended to suggest ways of structuring your discussions. Feel free to select what suits your group. The main goals of this lesson are to get to know the Gospel of Mark in general and the people with whom you are going to study it.

If you read through the entire Gospel of Mark this week, this may be the most time-consuming lesson for you to prepare. The group leader should warn members to allow several hours for reading Mark and doing the lesson. If reading the whole book is an impossible demand on someone's time, he or she could probably get a general impression of the Gospel by skimming portions of it for the story line and repeated ideas.

Worship. Some groups like to begin with prayer and/or singing. Some pray only briefly for God's guidance at the beginning, but leave extended prayer until after the study.

Warm-up. The beginning of a new study is a good time to lay a foundation for honest sharing of ideas, for getting comfortable with one another, and for encouraging a sense of common purpose. One way to establish common ground is to talk about what each group member hopes to get out of your group—out of your study of Mark, and out of any prayer, singing, sharing, outreach, or anything else you might do together. You can include what you hope to give to the group as well. If you have someone write down each member's hopes and expectations, then you can look back at these goals later to see if they are being met. You can then plan more time for prayer or decide to cover Mark more slowly if necessary.

You may decide to take about fifteen minutes at the beginning of your discussion of Lesson One to discuss goals. Or, you may prefer to take a whole meeting to hand out study guides, introduce the study, examine the "How to Use This Study" section on pages 5–8, and discuss goals.

First impressions. From Lesson One you should get, above all, first impressions of the book's themes and purposes on which to build deeper discoveries later. To focus your discussion, each group member might choose one event or teaching that was especially meaningful to him or her, and explain why. Ask the group to describe Jesus briefly. This open sharing could help introduce members who do not know each other well.

You need not compare the outlines of Mark's Gospel people might have made (question 3); these are for each student's personal use. You will want to share briefly first impressions (question 1), key terms (question 2), and the meaning of Mark 1:1 (question 4).

Application. If application is unfamiliar to some group members, choose a sample paragraph from the Gospel of Mark and discuss possible ways of applying it. Try to state specifically how the passage is relevant to you and how you might act in light of it. Think of responses that you might actually do, not just ideal responses (or something that "someone else" should do!). Do not forget that praying for ability, courage, discipline and/or guidance to do something is an appropriate application of a passage.

Give the group a chance to voice any questions about the book or its historical background. You may decide to postpone answering some questions until you deal with the relevant passage, but you can keep the group's questions in mind.

As you go through each lesson, you will notice that while a few application questions are included (as well as the "Optional Application" questions in the margins), most questions deal with the content of the Gospel. If there is no application question that relates to a question or concern that interests you, don't let that stop you from doing your own application! The relative scarcity of application questions in some lessons is not meant to de-emphasize the need to apply

Scripture to our lives, but rather to emphasize that we need to come to terms with the content of the Gospel before we can apply it.

Wrap-up. The wrap-up is a time to bring the discussion to a focused end and to make any announcements about the next lesson or meeting. For example, some lessons cover more material and include more questions than others. Prior to such a longer lesson, you may wish to decide whether you should cover it in two meetings.

Worship. Praise God for His wisdom in giving us four Gospels, and especially the Gospel of Mark, almost certainly the first of the four written. Praise Him for what He reveals about Himself in this book. Ask Him to help you "see Him more clearly, follow Him more nearly, and love Him more dearly" in all you do through your study of Mark's Gospel.

The Kingdom of God:
Already But Not Yet

"One dare not think he or she can properly interpret the Gospels without a clear understanding of the concept of the kingdom of God in the ministry of Jesus."[1] This may sound like strong language, but it is true.

The Jews whom Jesus addressed believed they lived at the brink of the end of "this age" and the beginning of "the age to come." They were waiting for the Messiah, who would usher in the age to come, the prophesied time when God would defeat all evildoers and rule the world with peace, justice, health, and prosperity. This time of God's rule was called "the Kingdom of God."

When John the Baptist announced that the Kingdom of God was at hand, people were on pins and needles waiting to see the Messiah appear and bring on the end. They expected the Messiah to be a warrior-king who would overthrow the evil Romans.When Jesus did the prophesied signs of the Messiah and the Kingdom—healing the sick, raising the dead, casting out demons—His disciples thought this was it: the age of righteousness was beginning. His crucifixion crushed them, but His

(continued on page 22)

21

(continued from page 21)
resurrection restored their hope that now, surely, He would bring the Kingdom to fulfillment.

However, by only a few months after the Resurrection, the disciples realized that Jesus had not come to usher in the "final" end, but the "beginning" of the end, as it were. Thus they came to see that with Jesus' death and resurrection, and with the coming of the Spirit, the blessings and benefits of the future had already come. In a sense, therefore, the end had already come. But in another sense the end had not yet fully come. Thus it was *already* but *not yet*.

The key to understanding Jesus' ministry and teaching is this tension between *already* and *not yet*. The Kingdom of God—the time of God's rule on earth—has come, but it has not fully come. The King has come, but He will come again. The citizens of the Kingdom live by the values and example of the King in a world that still lives very much by its own rules. They enjoy a foretaste of the Kingdom's peace, health, and freedom from sin, but await fulfillment of those benefits.

---

1. Gordon D. Fee and Douglas Stuart, *How to Read the Bible for All Its Worth* (Grand Rapids, MI: Zondervan, 1981, 1993), page 131. The discussion that follows is based on Fee and Stuart, pages 131-134.

MARK 1:1-45

The Coming
of the Kingdom

The prophetic voice in Israel had been silent for over
400 years, since the days of Malachi (about 400 BC).
Still, Israel longed for the everlasting Kingdom of righteousness promised to David by the prophet Nathan
(2 Samuel 7:12-16). The promise had been repeated
during seventy years of exile in Babylon: God would
deliver His people from bondage and establish His rule
of righteousness among His people.

Yet the years following the return of the Jews to
Jerusalem, the city of David, saw no Davidic kingdom
established. Instead, the people of Judea found themselves inhabitants of a vassal state. For over five hundred years, with the exception of a seventy-year inter-
lude of political independence, Judea remained under
the successive dominations of Persia (538–331 BC),
Greece (331–134 BC), and Rome (from 63 BC onward).
And even during that brief period of home rule (134–63
BC), Jerusalem hardly resembled the royal city of righteousness foretold by the prophets. Instead, the ruling
family established a dynasty, complete with intrigue
and assassinations, which shocked and repelled many
of Jerusalem's devout citizens who were looking for the
Kingdom of God.

But now, during the reign of Tiberius Caesar
(about AD 30), the prophetic voice was once more heard
in the land of Judea: a voice crying, "Prepare the way of
the Lord!" (Mark 1:3). Read Mark 1 straight through,
and try to get a picture in your mind of Jesus in action.

For Further Study:
Mark 1:2 is a quote from Malachi 3:1; Mark 1:3 is from Isaiah 40:3. Look up each verse in its context. What is the Old Testament author's main point in each case? How do these original main points coincide with what Mark is trying to say?

For Further Study:
Compare Mark's account of John baptizing in the desert with those of Matthew (Matthew 3:1-12) and Luke (Luke 3:1-18). What do they add that Mark omits? How do Matthew and Luke differ from one another?

John baptizing in the desert (1:2-8)

Mark sees the gospel message as the fulfillment of God's promises in the Old Testament (1:2-3). The gospel is not a divine "surprise"; it is a part of God's plan of salvation which began with God's calling of Abraham (Genesis 12:1-3).

Desert (1:3,12). The Jews viewed the desert as the abode of evil spirits.

John (1:4). Luke tells us that John was the son of Elizabeth, a relative of Jesus' mother, Mary (Luke 1:36).

Baptism (1:4). During John's time, the Jews often administered baptism as a rite of purification for Gentiles who were converting to Judaism. John went one step further, preaching that Jews as well as Gentiles needed to be baptized, as a sign of their turning away from sin, in order to prepare for the coming of the Messiah. See also "The Kingdom of God" on page 20.

---

1. John's clothing was similar to that of the Old Testament prophet Elijah (2 Kings 1:8, Mark 1:6). What is the significance of this (Malachi 4:5-6)?

2. State in your own words what you think is the central theme of John's message (1:7-8).

John baptizes Jesus (1:9-11)

3. What does God say to Jesus in verse 11? State the meaning in your own words.

24

The temptation of Jesus (1:12-13)

4. What does Mark's reference to angels (1:13) tell us about Jesus' humanity?

Optional Application:
Has God ever driven you into a "desert" experience? Are you in one now? Why do you think He has done this? How do you believe He wants you to respond?

"The time has come" (1:14-15)

Time (1:15). The Greek word here refers not so much to a date on the calendar (chronological time) as it does to a decisive time when God acts in a special way. The fact that Jesus says that *the* time has come indicates that the decisive crisis-point in history has arrived. That crisis point is the coming of the Kingdom of God.

5. What would Jesus' hearers have understood Him to be saying when He said, "The time has come, and the Kingdom of God is at hand"?

6. How do you think Jesus' call for Israel to repent might have struck His hearers, with their Jewish notion of the Kingdom of God?

25

Optional Application:
The Jews expected their
Messiah to be a warrior-
king, but things did not
turn out as they antici-
pated. How has your
experience of life with
Jesus been different
from what you once
expected?

Optional Application:
Simon, Andrew, James
and John "immediately"
left their nets to follow
Jesus (1:16-20). What
might Jesus be calling
you to leave "immedi-
ately" in order to follow
Him more faithfully?

"Follow me" (1:16-20)

Simon and Andrew (1:16). John's Gospel indicates
that Jesus already knew these two fishermen (John
1:35-42) before the call Mark records here. Mark's
omission of this information underscores the
urgency of Jesus' call and the need for immediate
response.

James and John (1:19). The fact that Mark mentions
that their father Zebedee had "hired men" may
indicate that this family was somewhat wealthy—
perhaps more so than Simon and Andrew.

7. a. Why is Jesus' call to the fishermen so urgent that
they leave their nets immediately to follow Him?

_____

_____

_____

_____

b. Do you feel that same urgency applies today?
Why or why not?

_____

_____

_____

_____

Preaching, healing, casting out demons (1:21-45)

Sabbath (1:21). From the Hebrew word *shabat*, meaning "seven." This was the seventh day of the Jewish week, which began at sundown Friday and
ended at sundown Saturday. On this day God's
people were to cease from their labors (Exodus
20:8) and pause to reflect on the things of God,
especially the teaching of the Law at the local
synagogue.

Synagogue (1:21). From a Greek word meaning "to come together." The synagogue was the center of both worship and education in the Jewish towns of Jesus' day. In Gentile cities, a synagogue could be started by as few as ten adult Jewish males.

Teachers of the Law (1:22). Other translations use "scribes." They were the scholars of the day, professionally trained in the interpretation and application of the Old Testament and the oral traditions handed down by generations of rabbis. They relied heavily on precedent (e.g., "Rabbi Hillel says such-and-such") for their authority.

Authority (1:22,27). In contrast to the scribes, Jesus needed no authority other than His own person. In addition, He cast out demons by the power of His own personal, direct command. This was in contrast to the Jewish exorcists of His day, who generally required a long ritual to invoke the power of God in order to free a demon-possessed person.

Leprosy (1:40). The word was used in biblical times to designate a wide variety of serious skin diseases. It is not limited to what we know as leprosy (Hansen's disease). Such diseases were thought highly contagious, and the Law of Moses commanded that lepers must remain isolated from the community while sick, and present sacrifices of cleansing if cured (see Leviticus 13–14 for the laws concerning leprosy).

8. What was the difference between Jesus' teaching and that of the "teachers of the law" whom the people were used to hearing (1:22)?

9. According to the demon-possessed man (1:23-24), who was Jesus and why had He come?

27

For Thought and Discussion: Why do you think Jesus did not want the demons to reveal that He was the Messiah (1:25,34)?

For Further Study: See Leviticus 13–14 for the Mosaic laws concerning leprosy and the treatment of lepers. Compare these with Jesus' treatment of the leper in Mark 1:40-42.

Optional Application: Do you ever feel so "unclean" that you don't think Jesus would reach out and touch you? Remember how Jesus healed the leper, even though the Law of Moses told the Jews not to touch lepers, and pray that He will touch you as well.

10. After preaching and healing in one town and before heading for another, what did Jesus do (1:35)? Why do you think He needed to do this?

_____

_____

_____

_____

_____

11. What does Jesus' interaction with the leper tell you about His character (1:40-42)?

_____

_____

_____

_____

_____

12. Why do you think Jesus urged the leper to tell no one how he was cured (1:43-45)?

_____

_____

_____

_____

13. What's your impression of Jesus as a person from what you've read so far?

_____

_____

_____

_____

_____

14. Summarize how people respond to Jesus' ministry throughout Mark 1:16-45.

_____

_____

_____

_____

_____

For the group

Warm-up. Ask each person to respond in a few sentences to the question, "What is the gospel?"

Read aloud. Have a good reader in the group read the first chapter of Mark to the entire group.

Summarize. Ask someone to give a brief overview (no more than two minutes) of what chapter one is about. Save any detailed commentary for group discussion.

Prepare the way of the Lord. Consider whether Mark 1:1 is an introduction to verses 2-8, or a title for the entire Gospel of Mark. Point to the possible parallel with Genesis 1:1 ("In the beginning . . ."). If Mark 1:1 is a title for the entire book, what does this tell us about Mark's view of the gospel of Jesus Christ?

Point out the implied comparison Mark makes between John and Elijah. What was the role Elijah was to fulfill in the last days, according to the Old Testament?

The baptism and temptation of Jesus. Consider why the sinless Jesus had to be baptized by John.

Be sure to emphasize that it was the Holy Spirit who "drove" Jesus into the desert to do spiritual battle with Satan. Does this fit in with group members' ideas about "spirituality" or the "Spirit-filled life"?

Preaching, healing and casting out demons. Ask group members if Jesus meets any opposition from 1:16 to the end of the chapter. If they say "none," refer them to 1:24. The fact that only the demons opposed His early ministry should tell us something about the opposition He receives later on, beginning in chapter 2.

Mark describes Jesus' ministries of healing and casting out demons, but says virtually nothing about the content of Jesus' preaching or teaching in chapter one. Why do you think Mark centers on Jesus' acts and not His words?

Application. Use the Optional Application questions, plus any other ideas from the group, to discern how God might be speaking to group members through Mark's Gospel. Be sure that you understand the meaning of the text (i.e., what Mark intended to say to his original readers) before trying to apply it. Otherwise, you run the risk of reading your own thoughts and circumstances into the text.

Wrap-up. Have each person answer the following question: "What one thing do I know now that I did not know before studying this chapter?"

Worship. Close in prayer, thanking God for what you have learned and asking God for wisdom to apply it during the coming week. If your group feels comfortable with "sentence prayers" by group members at this stage, encourage them to pray in this way, with the group leader designated to say the final prayer.

MARK 2:1–3:6

Opposition to the King

Chapter 1 of Mark's Gospel is a string of success stories. Jesus called men to follow Him, and they did so immediately. He preached, and the people flocked to hear Him. He healed the sick and exercised authority over the powers of darkness. His popularity was such that He could not even travel freely in public—yet the crowds still came to see Him (1:45).

Beginning in chapter 2, however, opposition began to develop. As Jesus began to speak more freely about the meaning of His message and the significance of His healing ministry, He provoked confrontation by challenging not only the authority of the religious leaders, but their whole way of life. Even at this early juncture, Mark saw storm clouds gathering over Jesus.

Read 2:1–3:6, observing the kinds of issues that raised controversy.

Jesus forgives sins (2:1-12)

Roof (2:4). The roof of the average house was flat and made with wood beams covered with brushwood and clay. It was therefore easy to take this roof apart or make a hole in it. A stairway usually led up the side of the house to the roof.

---

1. What motivated Jesus to respond to the paralytic's plight was his friends' *faith* (2:5). Why do you suppose their faith made such a difference to Jesus?

31

For Thought and Discussion: a. When Mark says Jesus saw "their faith" (2:5), is he referring to (1) the faith of the paralytic's friends, or (2) the faith of both the paralytic and his friends? Explain your answer.
  b. Was the faith Jesus recognized (2:5) necessary for forgiveness of sins? Why or why not?

Optional Application: Jesus simultaneously forgave the paralytic's sins and freed him from his paralysis. What sorts of sins may psychologically or spiritually "paralyze" us? Is there any such "paralysis" in your life from which you might be freed if you asked Jesus to forgive you?

2. Why do you think Jesus told the paralytic, "your sins are forgiven"?

_____

_____

_____

_____

Blaspheming (2:7). The Jews viewed blasphemy, the slander of God's name and reputation, as the greatest of sins. For a mere man to claim authority to forgive sins constituted such slander, since only God had such authority. In Jewish teaching even the Messiah could not forgive sins.[1]

Son of Man (2:10). Jesus used this title frequently to refer to Himself. It was a Hebrew expression that usually meant simply "man" (see, for example, Ezekiel 2:1,3; 3:1,3,4). In Jesus' day, however, it had also become a Messianic title. This usage of "Son of Man" was based upon Daniel 7:13-14, where the prophet Daniel saw a vision of "one like a son of man" (that is, one who looked like a man) coming down from Heaven to establish an ever-lasting Kingdom of righteousness on earth. On the basis of this passage, some Jews looked for the Messiah to appear not as an earthly political ruler such as King David, but rather as a heavenly being who would intervene supernaturally at the end of the age to judge the nations and save His people. The irony of a Galilean peasant using this title would not have been lost on the religious leaders of Jesus' day.

3. Up to this point, Jesus had been "preaching the word" to the people (2:2), not performing healings. Why, then, did He heal this one man (2:10)?

_____

_____

_____

_____

Jesus fraternizes with sinners (2:13-23)

Tax collectors (2:15). Instead of sending their own people to collect taxes, the Romans hired locals to do it on a contract basis. Contractors agreed to pay Rome a certain quota; anything they collected above this quota was theirs to keep. Needless to say, this system provided each tax collector with a strong incentive to collect as much as he could from the local residents—and many did just that. In addition, the Jews viewed any countryman of theirs who chose this lucrative profession as a collaborator with the forces of Rome which occupied Palestine, and therefore as a traitor. Tax collectors such as Levi were therefore regarded as social outcasts.

Sinners (2:15). The Pharisees applied this name to almost anyone who did not follow their own strict religious regimen.

Pharisees (2:16). A Jewish religious party which believed that strict obedience to the Law of Moses was the key to spiritual renewal for Israel. While members were usually laymen, a few were trained scribes (Mark 2:16) and thus had official status as religious leaders. Though few in number (generally estimated at 6,000, or roughly one percent of the Jewish population in Palestine during Jesus' day), they had a significant impact upon first-century Jewish society. The Pharisees were religious separatists and thus saw themselves as superior to the average Jewish citizen, yet they were generally respected—though not necessarily loved—by their countrymen. In their zeal to obey the Law of Moses they formulated a

33

lengthy catalog of interpretations that detailed precisely what was lawful and what was not, and regarded these interpretations as just as authoritative as the Law of Moses itself.

4. What did Levi stand to lose by leaving his work and following Jesus (2:14)?

_____

_____

_____

_____

5. Why do you think people of ill repute were so attracted to Jesus (2:15)?

_____

_____

_____

_____

6. This story reflects another disagreement between Jesus and the religious establishment. Try to put yourself on both sides of the debate.

a. From the Pharisees' point of view, why would it be bad for a rabbi to eat with people of ill repute?

_____

_____

_____

_____

b. From Jesus' point of view, why was it necessary that He do so?

_____

_____

_____

c. In what way(s) is this story relevant to us?

_____

_____

_____

_____

_____

A new order for the ages (2:18-22)

Fasting (2:18). Deliberate and sustained abstinence from all food for a specific period of time (usually one day). Jewish religious fasts were generally regarded as periods of penance or mourning.

Bridegroom (2:19). The Old Testament pictures God as the bridegroom, or husband, of His people Israel (Isaiah 54:5-8, Jeremiah 31:32, Ezekiel 16:1-13, Hosea 2:18-20).

7. In your own words, why didn't Jesus' disciples fast?

_____

_____

_____

8. To what does Jesus refer when He says the bridegroom will be taken away (2:20)?

_____

_____

_____

9. Where does this leave us? Should we celebrate because the bridegroom is here, fast because He is gone, or both?

_____

_____

_____

New wine (2:22). Newly made wine was placed in fresh leather wineskins where it fermented, thus causing the wineskins to expand. If such "new wine" were placed in wineskins previously used and thus fully stretched out and brittle, the old skins would burst under the pressure of the fermenting new wine.

---

10. Jesus tells two short parables (2:21-22) to make one point.

a. What do the old garment and the old wineskins represent?

_____

_____

b. What do the patch of unshrunk cloth and the new wine represent?

_____

_____

c. What are the new wineskins, and why are they needed?

_____

_____

_____

Lord of the Sabbath (2:23-28)

11. David broke the Law of Moses concerning the holy bread. Jesus' disciples broke the Pharisees' interpre-

tation of the Law concerning the Sabbath (the Pharisees said picking even a few grains counted as work, which was forbidden on the Sabbath). In your own words, tell why both David and Jesus' disciples were justified in breaking the Law.

Optional Application: Can you think of a time when the requirements of your Christian faith appeared to conflict with human need (2:23-28)? How did you respond? Do you think you responded correctly?

For Thought and Discussion: What significance do you see in the fact that the Pharisees were willing to plot with their archenemies, the Herodians, as to how they might do away with Jesus (3:6)?

12. Why do you suppose Jesus says that He is "Lord *even* of the Sabbath" (2:28)?

_____

_____

_____

_____

Deadly enemies (3:1-6)

Herodians (3:6). Probably influential Jews who were friends and supporters of Herod Antipas, who ruled Galilee as a puppet of the Roman government. Under normal circumstances, the Herodians were despised by the strictly orthodox, nationalistic Pharisees. See further note on Mark 6:14 (lesson 7, page 71).

13. What was it about the Pharisees' attitude that so distressed Jesus (3:5)?

_____

_____

_____

_____

For Further Study:
Make a list of how Jesus and the Pharisees differ in their response to each situation recorded in Mark 2:1–3:6. What does this tell us about the nature of true spirituality versus counterfeit spirituality?

14. The account of Jesus healing on the Sabbath (3:1-6) is the last of five consecutive "conflict" stories. Summarize the religious leaders' reasons for opposing Jesus.

_____

_____

_____

_____

15. Why do you think Mark placed all these accounts in one section?

_____

_____

_____

_____

16. List any questions you have about this section.

_____

_____

_____

_____

For the group

Worship.

Warm-up. Ask each group member to respond to the following: "When you find yourself in conflict with someone, do you most often (a) avoid the issue, (b) have a rational discussion about the issue, (c) argue about the issue, or (d) handle the conflict in some other way?"

Read aloud and summarize.

Opposition to the King. Whereas in chapter 1 Jesus gained many followers, in chapter 2 He makes a number of powerful enemies. The group should note the following:

1. Whereas in chapter 1 Jesus confronted the demons, in chapter 2 He begins to confront respected people within the Jewish religious community who were acting in ways contrary to Jesus' vision of the Kingdom of God. It's easier to confront obvious evil than to point out religious practices which may seem godly, but which in fact are contrary to the will of Christ. Ask group members to give examples of this.

2. Whereas chapter 1 emphasizes Jesus' mighty works, chapter 2 begins to spell out the meaning of those works: that is, the need for all people to turn from sin and toward Christ for forgiveness. Point out especially how Mark 2:1-12 makes it clear that Jesus' ministry of physical healing is of secondary importance to His primary mission of forgiving sins.

A new order. Compare the Pharisees' view of piety as a religious *fast* with Jesus' depiction of Christian discipleship as a wedding party (2:18-22). How does that fit with your view of what it means to be a Christian?

Lord of the Sabbath. Note how the Sabbath, originally intended by God as a means for His people to refresh themselves for obedience to Him ("The Sabbath was made for man"), became an end in itself ("man for the Sabbath") under the hair-splitting legalism of the Pharisees. Ask group members if they can think of instances in the Church today where commands originally intended as means to a good end have become ends in themselves.

Summary and application.

Wrap-up. In closing, refocus the group on the central theme Mark is trying to convey in 2:1–3:6: the Kingdom which Christ brings inevitably creates conflict with some of our most cherished notions of piety—especially the notion that we can earn God's favor by our own righteousness (2:17).

Make any brief remarks you wish about next week's lesson—for example, how Jesus' conflict with the authorities will intensify to the point that even His own family will think He's gone mad.

Worship. Close in prayer, thanking God that Jesus cares enough for us to confront us with those areas in our lives which need to be transformed by the power of the gospel. Encourage group members to focus on one such area in each of their lives, and to trust Christ to bring healing to it.

Since this is early in our study of Mark, some group members may not feel free to pray aloud about such concerns. Be sure to allow individuals the freedom to share with the group as they feel ready to do so. As members begin to feel such freedom, encourage prayer for one another within the group.

1. Walter W. Wessel, *Mark*, in *The Expositor's Bible Commentary*, vol. 8 (Grand Rapids, MI: Zondervan, 1984), page 633.

MARK 3:7-35

The Conflict Widens

Jesus' fame spread like wildfire beyond the bounds of His Galilean homeland. The power of His message was confirmed by signs and wonders, drawing people from as far away as Idumea to the south and the port cities of Tyre and Sidon to the north.

Yet as His popularity increased, so did the controversy surrounding His ministry. Religious leaders from Jerusalem, the seat of spiritual authority in Israel, journeyed northward to confront the challenge Jesus presented to their way of life. And even Jesus' own family saw Him as a stumbling block.

In the midst of the widening conflict, Jesus refused to retreat. Instead, He moved swiftly to widen His influence by appointing twelve select followers to minister in His name. Read 3:7-35.

Followers from far off (3:7-12)

The lake (3:7). The sea of Galilee. Capernaum, Peter's hometown and Jesus' "home away from home" (see 2:1), was located on its north shore. In the Bible, "the sea" is sometimes used to refer to the Gentile nations (e.g., Revelation 13:1)—an appropriate imagery in this verse, as Jesus is followed by crowds that include people from miles away in Gentile cities such as *Tyre* and *Sidon*.

1. Mark 3:8 is the first mention of people from outside Israel coming to hear Jesus. How does this

contribute to Mark's purpose in writing his Gospel (see page 12).

_____

_____

_____

2. Why do you think Jesus did not want the demons announcing that He was the Messiah ("the Son of God," 3:11-12)?

_____

_____

_____

_____

Jesus chooses the Twelve (3:13-19)

Twelve (3:14). The Old Testament nation of Israel was divided into twelve tribes. In choosing twelve apostles, Jesus was laying the foundation for a new, "spiritual" Israel—the Church (see Matthew 19:28, Galatians 6:16).

Apostles (3:14). The Greek *apostello* means "to send." Here it signifies one sent out with full authority to act on behalf of another. Following Jesus' resurrection and ascension, the term *apostle* took on a more specialized meaning, i.e., one who was both an eyewitness to the risen Jesus and specifically commissioned by Jesus as an agent of divine revelation (see Matthew 28:19, Acts 1:21-22, 1 Corinthians 9:1, Galatians 1:15-17).[1]

Zealot (3:18). The four major religious parties of Jesus' day were the Pharisees, Sadducees, Essenes, and Zealots. Like the Pharisees, Zealots believed in strict obedience to the Mosaic Law and the rabbinic traditions. Unlike the Pharisees, however, the Zealots' "zeal for the law" extended to armed insurrection in order to overthrow the occupying forces of Rome and establish the "Kingdom of God." Since Rome possessed such overwhelming military might, the Zealots avoided direct confrontation with the Roman forces in Palestine, instead relying on terrorist tactics such as political assassination.

Some Zealot leaders were messianic pretenders, such as the two insurrectionists, Theudas and Judas of Galilee, mentioned by the rabbi Gamaliel in Acts 5:36-37. The Zealots were also the key instigators of the Jewish revolt of AD 66, which ended with Roman armies destroying Jerusalem four years later.[2]

The fact that Jesus chose Simon the Zealot along with Matthew the tax collector (the same person as Levi; see Mark 2:14 and Matthew 9:9), whom Simon and many other Jews would have regarded as a collaborator with Rome, no doubt made for some lively discussions among the Twelve!

Iscariot (3:19). Probably derived from the Hebrew *Ish Kerioth,* or "man from Kerioth," a town in Judea. Judas seems to have been the only one of the Twelve from the providence of Judea—which may explain why he was more predisposed than were his eleven Galilean companions to turn Jesus over to the religious authorities in Jerusalem.

For Thought and Discussion: Jesus chose the Twelve in the midst of great opposition and controversy. What sort of a declaration was Jesus making to His enemies by choosing and commissioning the Twelve (3:14-15)?

Optional Application: The call of Jesus Christ brought together former archenemies like Matthew the tax collector and Simon the Zealot (3:16,18). How has Christ changed your attitudes toward people, or groups of people, with whom you previously did not associate? What changes in attitude do you feel still need to be made?

3. Jesus chose as apostles both Simon the Zealot and Matthew the tax collector. What does this say to you about Jesus' view of the Kingdom of God?

_____

_____

_____

Spiritual warfare (3:20-30)

4. Jesus' family thought He was crazy (3:21). Put yourself in their position and discuss how you might have felt under similar circumstances.

_____

_____

43

For Thought and Discussion: Jesus' family heard about His ministry and thought He was crazy (3:21). What reasons might they have had for thinking this way? List as many possible reasons as you can think of.

For Further Study: Jesus saw His primary conflict being not with other people, but with Satan and the demons (Mark 3:27). Paul says the same thing about the Christian life in Ephesians 6:10-19. Read this passage, then make a list of the spiritual resources Paul says we need to fight the "principalities and powers" (Satan and the demons), adding any comments or questions you may have as you write them down.

Optional Application: Jesus regarded Satan and the demons as personal, malevolent spirit-beings, and not as mere manifestations of physical or psychological disorders. Do you believe it makes a difference in our spiritual lives whether or not we have the same view of demons as did Jesus? Why, or why not?

———————————————

———————————————

———————————————

———————————————

Beelzebub (3:22). From the Hebrew, meaning "Lord of flies." The origin of the term is uncertain (but clearly derogatory); however, the context makes it clear that Beelzebub and Satan (3:23) were to the Jewish mind one and the same: the prince of darkness, lord of the demons. Also spelled *Beelzebul* or *Bezebul*.

5. The Jewish leaders who criticized Jesus (3:22) had come all the way from Jerusalem to Galilee. What significance do you attach to this?

———————————————

———————————————

———————————————

6. In your own words, how did Jesus refute His opponents' accusation that He was in league with the Devil (3:23-26)?

———————————————

———————————————

———————————————

7. In 3:24-25, Jesus discusses the kingdom of Satan. However, what do these verses tell you about Jesus' view of the Kingdom of God?

———————————————

———————————————

44

8. From the context (3:23-30), what do you think is the "blasphemy of the Holy Spirit" of which Jesus speaks in 3:29?

_____

_____

_____

_____

9. Why do you think Jesus regarded this sin as uniquely worthy of divine judgment?

_____

_____

_____

_____

"Who are my brothers?" (3:31-35)

Jesus' mother and brothers (3:31). The word *brothers* could be generic, referring also to sisters. Mark 6:3 notes that Jesus had at least four brothers. One of these, James, later became leader of the church in Jerusalem (Acts 15) and was known as "James the just," according to the Jewish historian Josephus.

No mention is made of Jesus' father, Joseph. Indeed, none of the four Gospel writers states that Joseph was alive during Jesus' ministry (note that in 6:3 Mark calls Jesus "Mary's son"—highly unusual terminology in Jewish culture, especially if Joseph were still living).

According to Matthew 1:6-16, Joseph was a legal heir to David's throne, and therefore to the "Kingdom of God" expected by the Jews. It is therefore likely that in God's providence Joseph died before Jesus began His ministry, thereby leaving Jesus as legal heir to the Davidic Kingdom.

For Thought and Discussion: Mark records three principal activities in Jesus' ministry: preaching, healing, and casting out demons. Which of these three is the primary evidence that the Kingdom of God has arrived in the Person of Jesus? Why? Compare Matthew 12:28 and Luke 11:20.

For Thought and Discussion: a. Who is the "strong man" of whom Jesus speaks (3:27)? Who is the robber?

b. What, then, is the true significance ("in fact," 3:27) of Jesus' ministry of casting out demons?

For Thought and Discussion: Do you believe it is possible for a Christian to commit the "unforgivable sin" (Mark 3:29)?

45

10. Mark has already said why Jesus' family came to Him (3:21). Why do you think Mark places the account of Jesus and Beelzebub in between the departure of Jesus' family (3:21) and their arrival in Capernaum (3:31)?

_____

_____

_____

_____

_____

11. a. In Mark 3:34-35, who specifically are those who are doing God's will?

_____

_____

b. How were those people doing God's will (as distinct from the Pharisees, who believed that by obeying the Law of Moses, as they understood it, they were doing God's will)?

_____

_____

_____

_____

12. Summarize the progression of Jesus' ministry from Mark 2:1 through 3:35. Why do you think Mark ends this section with the story of Jesus' family coming to take Him away?

_____

_____

_____

_____

_____

_____

13. List any questions you have about this section.

_____

_____

_____

For the group

Warm-up. Have each person briefly share one instance, either in his own life or the life of a friend, when faithfulness to Christ resulted in conflict with others.

Read aloud and summarize.

Followers from far off; Jesus chooses the Twelve.
Point out to the group how Mark portrays the widening scope of Jesus' ministry. Gentiles now come from afar to hear Him (3:7-8), and Jesus responds by choosing twelve men to be with Him and minister in His name (3:14-15). This is the first instance of Jesus working through others. Discuss the significance of Jesus working through His followers for your lives as people who follow Him.

Spiritual warfare. The Jewish teachers who oppose Jesus begin to send envoys all the way from Jerusalem to contradict Jesus' radical claims to divine authority (3:22). The absurd accusations brought forth against Jesus by the teachers of Jerusalem, plus the presence of Gentile followers (3:8), underscore Jesus' parable of the "new wine" uttered in the previous chapter.

Recall from lessons 1 and 2 what sort of "Kingdom of God" the people of Israel were expecting. Compare and contrast their expectations with the sort of kingdom Jesus alludes to in 3:22-27. A discussion about the reality of spiritual warfare would be appropriate here.

Some group members may wonder if they have committed the "eternal sin" (3:29-30). Be sure to call

47

attention to the specific context of Jesus' remark, noting that He is not addressing Christians, but unbelievers who use desperate personal attacks to discredit Him because they cannot refute either His words or His works.

"Who are my brothers?" For first-century Jews, the family was central to their way of life. Keep this in mind as you discuss the significance of Jesus' words in 3:34-35 for your commitment to Christ, and your commitment to fellow Christians.

Summarize.

Wrap-up. Review the progression of Jesus' ministry in lessons 2 through 4, noting the simultaneous increase both in His popularity and in the animosity He arouses. Encourage group members to keep Mark 1–3 in mind as they read Mark 4:1-34 for next week's lesson.

Worship.

1. Oscar Cullmann, *Peter: Disciple-Apostle-Martyr* (New York: Meridian Books, 1958), page 216.
2. Martin Hengel, *Was Jesus a Revolutionist?* (Philadelphia: Fortress Press, 1971), pages 10-14.

MARK 4:1-34

The Mystery of the Kingdom of God

Even as Jesus preached to great crowds and sought to widen His influence through the twelve apostles whom He had chosen (3:13-19), He simultaneously began to shift His strategy by directing most of His teaching to those who followed Him most closely. He was no doubt aware that many who followed Him were more interested in His healing ministry and anti-establishment tone than in the meaning of His message. It is probably fair to say that Jesus' enemies understood His message better than did many of those who flocked to see Him.

For this reason Jesus began to concentrate on developing the faith of His disciples, spending less time with the crowds and more with the Twelve and other close followers. In line with this, He began to use parables as a teaching device. Such simple stories, which contained profound truths dressed in everyday garb, made it necessary for His audience to listen very carefully and ponder the meaning of His words. In this way only those most committed to Jesus would gain further understanding of the Kingdom of God which He preached. Read 4:1-34.

Parable of the sower (4:1-9)

Study Skill—Interpreting Parables
The word *parable* comes from the Greek *parabole*, which signifies something which is "set alongside" something else in order to make a comparison

(continued on page 50)

49

(continued from page 49)
between the two. The parables of Jesus come in many forms, including stories, riddles, and even jokes. In each case Jesus talks about something with which His listeners are familiar, then "sets it alongside" the spiritual truth He seeks to communicate.

The parables in Mark 4:1-34 all center around the theme of the Kingdom of God (4:11). As we seek to understand them, the following points should be kept in mind:

1. A parable is designed to communicate one central truth. It differs from an allegory in that not every detail of the parable needs to have a "spiritual" meaning. For example, in the parable of the mustard seed (Mark 4:30-32) one ought not to seek a "spiritual meaning" for details such as the tree branches and the birds. Such details are "window dressing" to enliven the parable, so that the main point will be driven home with greater impact.

Jesus did attach meaning to certain details in some of His parables, the best example being the Parable of the Sower (see Mark 4:14-20). Even there, however, He did not seek to define every detail (the sun, for example). When interpreting a parable, then, we should take care not to press every detail too far, unless (a) the meaning is clear from the immediate context, or (b) Jesus Himself interprets the details.

2. The one central truth of a parable often calls for a response. For example, the Parable of the Sower (which may more accurately be called the Parable of the Soils) confronts Jesus' listeners with the question, "What sort of soil are *you*? How will you respond to the coming of the Kingdom of God?"

3. Since a parable refers to events and experiences familiar to its original audience (in this case, first-century Palestinian farmers), the modern-day interpreter must know something of the culture back then in order to grasp the full impact of the message.

4. The parables are not "eternal truths" dropped down from heaven, but rather teaching devices addressed to specific situations. They must therefore be read in light of His ministry, and not as general religious or moral maxims which have meaning apart from His person and work. *(continued on page 51)*

(continued from page 50)

5. A parable seeks to communicate truth *indirectly*. In so doing it requires the listener to ponder the meaning of the story, rather than giving the meaning directly.

At times, Jesus' disciples could understand a parable only by asking Jesus for its meaning (Mark 4:10). Many other listeners did not bother to ask Jesus about the parables, however. Thus, Jesus used parables not merely as a device to communicate a message, but also as a catalyst to draw people to Himself. To those who responded by following Him, He gave further insight. To those who did not inquire further into the meaning of the parables of the Kingdom, Jesus' words remained clever stories, but little more (Mark 4:11).

1. Mark's first reference to Jesus teaching "in parables" (4:2) comes immediately after opposition to Jesus has reached such a point that even His relations with His family are strained (3:21,31-35). Why do you think Jesus would pick this time to begin using parables, as opposed to proclaiming His message more directly?

_____

_____

_____

_____

The farmer (4:3). In first-century rural Palestine, farmers sowed seed by scattering it in handfuls all over the ground, rather than carefully in rows, as we do today. "The sower deliberately sowed on the path (v. 4), in rocky places (v. 5), and among the thorns (v. 7) because sowing preceded plowing. However, if plowing was delayed for any time at all, the consequences Jesus mentioned inevitably resulted."[1]

The path (4:4). The pathway in the field upon which the sower walked. The ground there was packed down tightly so that the seed which landed there lay on top of the ground in plain view of hungry birds.

51

Rocky places (4:5). Not soil with lots of stones mixed in, but rather portions of the farmer's field in which limestone bedrock lay close to the surface. In those areas there was little depth of soil, so that the seed could not put down deep roots. After the rainy season the hot sun dried up the ground quickly, thus scorching the shallow roots which had begun to grow during the rains.

Thorns (4:7). Even if the farmer had cut away the thorny plants in his field, the roots which remained could grow back so quickly that they would choke out the growth from any seeds scattered nearby.

Hear (4:9,23). In the Bible, hearing is the essential form by which the word of God is received.[2] Thus Jesus' call for His audience to "hear" is more than a call to listen carefully. It is a command to receive and obey His message.

2. The crowds to which Jesus spoke near the Sea of Galilee (4:1) were farmers who would have had no trouble understanding the details of a story about a man sowing seed in his field. Why, then, did Jesus assume that the crowds would have difficulty understanding His message (4:3,9)?

_____

_____

_____

_____

_____

Explaining the parable (4:10-20)

3. a. How did those closest to Jesus respond to the parables (4:10)?

_____

_____

_____

52

b. What about the crowds in general?

_____

_____

_____

Secret (4:11). The Greek word is *mysterion*, or "mystery."[3] It signifies not some esoteric doctrine which only a few are able to understand, but rather a truth heretofore concealed by God but now revealed by God to His people through the Gospel.

_____

4. Jesus explained the "secret" only to His disciples, and not to the crowds in general (4:11). Why do you think He did this?

_____

_____

_____

_____

5. In Mark 4:12 Jesus quotes Isaiah 6:9-10. In Isaiah 6:1-13, God told Isaiah to preach judgment upon Israel, giving Israel an opportunity to repent while knowing beforehand that Israel would reject the opportunity and that judgment would surely come. Why do you think Jesus considered Isaiah's words relevant to His preaching of the Kingdom of God?

_____

_____

_____

_____

6. Jesus said that the farmer sows "the word" (4:14). To what specific "word" is Jesus referring?

_____

_____

For Thought and Discussion: Jesus regarded the parable of the sower as the key to interpreting all of the other parables (4:13). What is the central idea it conveys upon which all the other "parables of the Kingdom" elaborate?

Optional Application: What "thorns" (4:18-19) have cropped up in your life within the last few years which threatened to "choke out" the fruit of spiritual growth? How did God deliver you from these thorns? (Or are you still battling them?!)

Optional Application:
Since the Kingdom of God has come in such a way that people can either accept or reject it (4:15-20), how should we feel toward someone who refuses to believe in Christ after we have witnessed to him or her?

Optional Application:
The growth of the seed depends on the quality of the soil. What can you do in your own life or in the life of another person to improve the quality of the soil?

7. In lesson 1 we saw that the Jews expected the Kingdom of God to come in spectacular, powerful fashion, and that no one would be able to resist it. How does this Jewish expectation of the Kingdom compare to the picture Jesus paints in Mark 4:14-20?

_____

_____

_____

_____

_____

8. a. According to Jesus, what are some obstacles which prevent people from accepting the gospel and persevering in faith (4:16-19)?

_____

_____

_____

_____

_____

b. List several specific actions Christians might take to overcome these obstacles.

_____

_____

_____

_____

_____

_____

_____

Listen! (4:21-25)

9. a. In Mark 4:24 Jesus urges His followers to "use" that which He has thus far "measured" out to them. What will happen if people "use," or put into practice, the word of Jesus? What of those who do not?

For Thought and Discussion: Who or what does the "lamp" (4:21) represent? When do you think the "hidden" (i.e., the full light of the lamp) will be revealed (4:22)?

_____

_____

_____

_____

_____

b. Write down one specific word of Jesus (a promise, a new truth, or a command) which you can use or apply in your life this week.

_____

_____

_____

_____

Parable of the grain (4:26-29)

Harvest (4:29). The Old Testament prophets used the grain harvest as a metaphor for the judgment that God would bring upon the earth at the end of the present evil age (Hosea 6:11, Joel 3:13). John the Baptist likewise depicted the final judgment as a harvest where the wheat would be separated from the chaff (Matthew 3:12).

10. Jesus likened the growth of the Kingdom of God to the slow, at times invisible, growth of a seed into mature grain.

a. How does this differ from the then-current Jewish expectation of the coming of the Kingdom?

For Thought and Discussion: Compare Mark 4:28 with 1 Corinthians 3:6-7. In your own words, what is our job? What is God's job?

For Further Study: In Jewish thought, the coming of the Kingdom of God would bring judgment as well as salvation. List the references to judgment and the references to salvation in Mark 4:3-32.

b. What encouragement, if any, do you find in this parable?

_____

_____

_____

_____

Parable of the mustard seed (4:30-32)

Mustard seed (4:31). "The smallest seed" known to the Galilean farmers in Jesus' audience, the seed from the mustard plant grows into a bush as high as ten feet—definitely large for a "garden plant"!

11. a. In your own words, state the meaning of this parable.

_____

_____

_____

b. How did it apply to Jesus' first disciples?

_____

_____

c. Many historians believe Mark wrote his Gospel to Christians being persecuted by the Roman state. How might this parable have encouraged them?

_____

_____

_____

_____

_____

d. Can you apply it to your situation?

_____

_____

_____

_____

_____

Timing (4:33-34)

12. Why do you think Jesus spoke only in parables to the crowds at this point in His ministry (4:33)?

_____

_____

_____

_____

13. Review the parables and see if you can detect a pattern to them. Did Mark put them in this particular order for a reason? If so, try to outline the flow of Mark's argument.

_____

_____

Optional Application:
What is the most signifi-
cant truth you have
learned in this week's
lesson? How will you
apply it to your life?

Optional Application:
What does Mark
4:33-34 teach that
might help you in shar-
ing the gospel with
nonChristian friends?

14. List any questions you have about this section.

For the group

Worship.

Warm-up. Ask each group member to make up a short
parable which begins "The Kingdom of God is like. . . ."
(As group leader, you must go first!) This exercise will
help each group member articulate his or her beliefs. It
will also demonstrate how hard it is to make up a good
parable!

Read aloud and summarize.

Parable of the sower; explaining the parable. The
group leader should emphasize that parables must be
interpreted against their historical background. It is
rather easy to "read into" a parable a meaning which
seems to fit, but has little to do with the point Jesus was
trying to make. For example, the parable of the lamp has
been interpreted as a general religious teaching that "the
truth cannot stay hidden forever."[4] This may (or may
not) be true, but we must remember that Jesus' parables
were always related to His specific ministry. Thus "that
which is hidden" most likely refers not to "truth" in general, but to the specific truth Jesus was teaching about
the Kingdom of God—or, to Jesus Himself.

Ask each group member to share his or her interpretation of the key parable of this lesson: the Parable

of the Sower. You might also discuss this statement by George Eldon Ladd, late professor of New Testament at Fuller Theological Seminary: "[the mystery] is that the Kingdom that is to come finally in apocalyptic power, as foreseen in Daniel, has in fact entered into the world in advance in a hidden form to work secretly within and among men."[5]

Listen!, the grain, the mustard seed. Discuss how these parables relate to the Parable of the Sower and to one another.

Timing. For Jesus, timing was crucial. He did not reveal the entire truth about Himself all at once, but was sensitive to what people were able to receive at any given point in their lives. Talk about the importance of being sensitive to God's timing in our lives, and in the lives of others.

Summarize.

Wrap-up. Encourage people to apply what they have learned, reminding them that while the Kingdom of God is already at work among us (4:14-20), it still remains to be consummated in all its fullness (4:22,29). How, then, are we called to live in the interim?

Worship. Encourage each group member to pray that the seed of God's Word might bear fruit in one specific area of his or her life this week.

1. Wessel, page 648.
2. Gerhard Kittel, editor, *Theological Dictionary of the New Testament*, Volume One (Grand Rapids, MI: Eerdmans, 1964), page 216.
3. Kittel, page 216.
4. See, for example, William Barclay, *The Gospel of Mark* (Philadelphia, PA: Westminster, 1956), page 98.
5. George E. Ladd, *A Theology of the New Testament* (Grand Rapids, MI: Eerdmans, 1974), page 94.

MARK 4:35–5:43

Signs and Wonders

The enigmatic character of Jesus' parables was matched by His unconventional ministry. As He healed the sick, Jesus claimed divine authority and deliberately violated the strict Sabbath regulations imposed by the Jewish religious leaders. At the same time, He preached a "Kingdom of God" unlike anything foreseen by His fellow Jews: not an earthly realm established by political force or apocalyptic divine intervention, but rather the reign of God in people's individual lives. Such a "Kingdom" could, and would, be resisted by many, but would nevertheless grow and accomplish God's purposes during the present evil age, until such time as God would bring final judgment to the nations of the earth.

Having preached the coming of God's Kingdom to fellow Jews in Galilee, Jesus now broke yet another religious barrier: He carried the gospel of God's salvation beyond the bounds of Israel into Gentile territory (Mark 5:1). In this way Jesus demonstrated that God's Kingdom would not be confined to one race or nation, but rather was extended to all who would turn from their sins and place their trust in Jesus. Read 4:35–5:43.

Stilling the storm (4:35-41)

The other side (4:35). Mark places Jesus' preaching of the parables on the western shore of the Sea of Galilee, probably near Capernaum (2:1). The eastern shore of the Sea of Galilee was populated largely by Gentiles (see notes on 5:11,20—this lesson, page 62).

For Thought and Discussion: Have you ever felt like the disciples did in Mark 4:38? How did God respond to your fear and frustration?

Optional Application: Mark 4:41 indicates that the disciples learned something new about Jesus' power after He had stilled the storm. Name one new truth you learned about Jesus this week, and write down how you plan to apply it to your life.

Furious squall (4:37). The Sea of Galilee is about 680 feet below sea level. Winds often come up suddenly from the surrounding hills, turning a placid lake into turbulent waves within minutes.

1. Contrast Jesus' behavior during the storm with that of His disciples (4:38).

2. What did the disciples learn about Jesus from this episode?

Legion (5:1-20)

Tombs (5:3). People in first-century Palestine were often buried in natural caves or in tombs cut out of the limestone rock. These provided good shelter for anyone desiring to live there. It was a natural place for a possessed man to dwell because of the popular belief that tombs were the favorite haunts of demons.[1]

Legion (5:9). A Roman legion consisted officially of six thousand soldiers, although the figure was rarely exact.

Pigs (5:11). The Law of Moses declared pigs to be an unclean animal (Leviticus 11:7-8). The fact that such a large herd was present in this region shows that many Gentiles lived there.

Decapolis (5:20). A confederation of ten cities located (with one exception) on the eastern shore of the

62

Sea of Galilee. *Decapolis* is Greek for "ten cities." The non-Hebrew name is yet another indicator of the fact that the area was predominantly Gentile.

3. Why were the demons so terrified of Jesus (5:7)?

_____

_____

_____

_____

4. Why do you think Jesus allowed the demons to go into the pigs (5:11-13)?

_____

_____

_____

_____

5. a. Discuss the reaction of the Gerasene people to Jesus' healing of the demoniac. Why do you think they were afraid of Jesus?

_____

_____

_____

_____

b. How do you think you might have reacted under similar circumstances?

_____

_____

_____

_____

6. a. Jesus did not permit this Gentile who had been possessed by demons to follow Him (5:19). Can

you think of any reasons why Jesus would not want this man to join those who were following Him?

_____

_____

_____

_____

_____

b. Compare Jesus' command to the former demoniac (5:19) with what the man actually did (5:20). How can this serve as an example for us?

_____

_____

_____

_____

Healing the sick, raising the dead (5:21-43)

Other side of the lake (5:21). Jesus and His disciples now return to Jewish territory, probably in or near Capernaum. Jesus' extension of His ministry to Gentiles does not preclude His continuing to minister to the Jews as well.

Synagogue rulers (5:22). Jairus was not a priest or scribe, but a layman whose responsibilities were administrative, including such things as looking after the building and supervising worship.[2]

Bleeding (5:25). Possibly due to some sort of uterine disease. Such bleeding was not only unhealthy and uncomfortable, but also left the woman ceremonially unclean (Leviticus 15:25-27), thus shutting her off from the worship of God and the fellowship of her friends.[3] Anyone whom she touched would have become unclean for a period of time as well.

7. What does Jairus's plea to Jesus (5:23) tell us about the strength of his faith? Why?

_____

_____

_____

_____

8. Compare the faith of the woman (5:28) with that of Jairus. Do you think her faith was greater than his? Why or why not?

_____

_____

_____

_____

9. Why do you think the woman was afraid to admit that she had touched Jesus (5:33)?

_____

_____

_____

_____

10. Does His reply to her (5:34) give comfort to you? If so, how?

_____

_____

_____

_____

_____

11. Read again Mark 5:35-36. Why do you think Jesus felt the need to exhort Jairus not to fear, but to believe (Mark 5:36)?

Optional Application: The woman who touched Jesus (5:25) believed in Him, but was also afraid of Him. Have you ever felt afraid of God? How can Jesus' words and deeds in Mark 4:35–5:43 help you overcome those fears?

For Thought and Discussion: Jesus felt power go out of Him as soon as the woman touched His garment and was healed (5:28-30). How do you think He "recharged His batteries" after such periods of strenuous ministry?

Optional Application: What do you fear in life? Write down one or two fears you have, and pray for wisdom as to how to deal with them.

12. This is Mark's first account of Jesus raising someone from the dead. Yet Jesus allowed only five
people to witness the event, and urged them not
to spread the news. Why do you think He did this?

13. Looking back over Mark 4:35–5:43, write down
those instances where Jesus responded to faith, and
those where His own actions created faith.

responded to faith	created faith

14. List any questions you have about this section.

For the group

Warm-up. Ask each group member this question: "Which person in this week's lesson do you most identify with, and why?"

Read aloud and summarize.

Stilling the storm. Point out that Jesus said to His disciples, "Let us go over to the other side" of the lake. It was His idea to take the boat across the Sea of Galilee. Still, the disciples found themselves unable to trust Him to get them across once the going got rough.

Have you ever been through an unexpected "storm" which caused you to forget that God has promised to take care of you? Discuss this question as a group, and look for ways to build up one another in faith.

Legion. Jesus' willingness to "cross the lake" and minister to Gentiles met with immediate opposition from the armies of Satan. What are some more subtle ways in which Satan tries to keep Christians from sharing the gospel of Christ with nonbelievers?

Healing the sick, raising the dead. Both the woman and Jairus had to overcome fears in order to exercise faith. Discuss the Optional Application question dealing with fear and faith.

Summarize.

Wrap-up. Note how Mark combined two main themes in 4:35–5:43: the spread of the gospel beyond the Jewish community, and the necessity of faith in Jesus Himself (and not simply in a message He preaches). These themes will be receiving increasing emphasis as we continue through Mark's Gospel.

Worship.

1. Wessel, *Mark* page 657.
2. Wessel, *Mark* page 660.
3. Barclay, *The Gospel of Mark*, page 128.

MARK 6:1-56

The Signs Continue

No longer content to let Gentiles from afar come to hear His message of the Kingdom (3:8), Jesus now ventured into Gentile territory and demonstrated that wherever He went, the power of the Kingdom of God vanquished the powers of Satan (5:1-20). Even the sting of death was defeated by the power of Jesus' word (5:41).

In His final tour of Galilee, Jesus continued to confront the powers of darkness, both directly and through His twelve apostles (6:7-13). He demonstrated His power not only as Lord over the demonic hosts, but even over creation itself (6:30-52). And people everywhere flocked to see Jesus. At the same time, faith was a much less common commodity among His listeners, especially those closest to Him: those of His hometown and those who followed Him wherever He went.

A prophet without honor (6:1-6)

His hometown (6:1). Jesus was raised in Nazareth, about twenty miles southwest of the Sea of Galilee (Matthew 2:23). The people of Nazareth had heard of their famous carpenter's miraculous exploits (Mark 6:2), although this was the first time He had visited His hometown to teach.

Judas (6:3). According to tradition, the author of the New Testament Epistle of Jude.

For Thought and Discussion: Have you ever tried to share the gospel with your family and/or closest friends, as did Jesus (Mark 6:1-6)? What was their response?

1. In your own words, describe the reaction of the people of Nazareth to Jesus' teaching ministry.

_____

_____

_____

2. Why do you think they reacted this way?

_____

_____

_____

_____

_____

3. What prevented Jesus from doing more than a few miracles (6:5) in Nazareth? Why do you think that made such a difference?

_____

_____

_____

_____

Sending out the Twelve (6:7-13)

Two by two (6:7). Apart from the advantages of companionship, the apostles went out in pairs so that the truthfulness of their testimony about Jesus might be established "on the testimony of two or three witnesses" (Deuteronomy 17:6).

4. Jesus told His disciples to "travel light" during their preaching mission. What do you think is the significance of this?

70

_____

_____

_____

_____

_____

_____

For Thought and Discussion: Review every instance in Mark 1–6 where Jesus or His disciples cast out demons. What does this activity tell you about why Jesus came?

5. What was the central activity of this mission (6:7,13), and what does this tell us about why Jesus came to earth?

_____

_____

_____

_____

_____

Optional Application: Jesus sent the Twelve on a specific mission. Do you sense God directing you to a specific ministry? Pray specifically for His guidance in this area.

Who is Jesus? (6:14-16)

King Herod (6:14). Herod Antipas, whose father, Herod the Great, tried to kill the infant Jesus (Matthew 2:16). When his father died, Antipas became tetrarch ("ruler of one-fourth") of Galilee and Perea.

Elijah (6:15). The first of a long line of prophets who spoke against Israel's idolatry following the division of David's and Solomon's kingdom in 931 BC. Elijah worked great miracles, and was considered the prototype of the prophets by the Jews of Jesus' day. In addition, the prophet Malachi predicted Elijah's return just prior to God's final judgment upon the world (Malachi 4:5).

6. People said many things about Jesus—but not that He was the Messiah (6:14-15). In your opinion,

71

For Further Study:
Compare Herod Antipas (Mark 6:16-27) with his father, Herod the Great (Matthew 2:1-12) and his nephew, Herod Agrippa I (Acts 12:1-4,19-23). List character traits you see as common to the Herodian dynasty.

Optional Application:
Herod's sin "snowballed" out of his control (6:16-27). What can you learn from his experience in order to prevent the same from occurring in your life?

what was there about Jesus' ministry that kept most people from believing that He was the Messiah?

_____

_____

_____

_____

Retrospective: Herod and John the Baptist (6:17-29)

Herodias (6:17). The daughter of Aristobulos, son of Herod the Great and half-brother of Antipas. Herodias was thus the niece of Antipas. Marriage to one's niece was permitted by the Law of Moses, but marriage to the wife of one's living brother was not (Leviticus 18:16). Herodias had divorced Philip to marry Antipas. The family of Herod was part Jewish and was, politically speaking, the royal house of Israel. John therefore saw them as subject to Mosaic Law.

Philip (6:17). Herod Philip, son of Herod the Great and another half-brother of Antipas. Herod Philip is not "Philip the tetrarch" mentioned in Luke 3:1.

7. a. Although Herod had great respect for John (6:20), yet he had John put to death (6:27). What motivated Herod to do this?

_____

_____

_____

b. What do Herod's actions throughout this episode show us about the way sin operates?

_____

_____

_____

_____

_____

8. How was John's condemnation of Herod's adulterous marriage (6:18) related to the central message of John's preaching (Mark 1:2-8)?

_____

_____

_____

_____

_____

Jesus feeds the 5,000 (6:30-44)

Eight months of a man's wages (6:37). Literally, "two hundred denarii." A denarius was the daily wage for a hired hand.

Loaves (6:38). John 6:9 tells us these were barley loaves. People would eat several of these small, flat pieces of bread at a single meal.

9. What does Jesus' reaction to the crowds (6:34) tell you about . . .

His character? _____

_____

_____

His mission? _____

_____

_____

10. Why do you think Jesus provided much more than enough food for the people, then had the surplus carefully gathered up (6:42-43)?

_____

_____

_____

_____

Jesus walks on the sea (6:45-52)

Bethsaida (6:45). A village on the northern shore of the Sea of Galilee, east of Capernaum.

Fourth watch (6:48). According to Roman custom, the night was divided into four "watches" of approximately three hours each. The fourth watch would be sometime between 3:00 a.m. and 6:00 a.m.

11. What were the disciples' two responses to seeing Jesus walk on the water (6:49-51)?

_____

_____

_____

_____

12. To what does Mark attribute the fact that they were "completely amazed" (6:51-52)?

_____

_____

13. Mark indicates that if the disciples had understood the significance of Jesus' feeding the 5,000, they would not have been surprised that Jesus walked on the sea or that the wind died down once He got into the boat (6:52). What do these three events tell us about Jesus?

_____

_____

_____

_____

Healing the multitudes (6:53-56)

Gennesaret (6:53). A village on the western shore of
the Sea of Galilee, or perhaps the general region in
which the village was located. The disciples evidently were blown off course from their original
heading toward Bethsaida.

14. Mark says "all who touched [Jesus] were healed"
(6:56). What does this tell you about these people's
attitude toward Jesus (compare 6:5-6)?

_____

_____

_____

15. Review Mark 6:1-56 and apply one new truth you
learned this week to a specific area of your life.

_____

_____

_____

_____

16. List any questions you have about this section.

_____

_____

_____

_____

For the group

Warm-up. If any group members have shared Christ both with strangers and with family members and close friends, ask them to share some of their experiences. Which was easier? Why?

Read aloud and summarize.

Questions. This chapter represents Jesus' last tour of Galilee before an extended trip into Gentile territory. Discuss with the group what Jesus does in this chapter that He did not do previously in Galilee, in order to make His last tour an effective one.

Have the group discuss how Jesus forced the disciples to depend on God's provision during their evangelistic travels (6:8-10). Also note that Jesus Himself said that those who rejected the disciples were in fact rejecting Him (6:11). What does this mean for us as witnesses to Jesus today?

Discuss the "Optional Application" regarding Herod's sin and how it "snowballed" out of control. Talk about positive steps Christians can take to keep this from happening in their lives.

Compare the miracles of Jesus feeding the 5,000 and His walking on the water, and take note of the disciples' response (6:52). As a group, try to identify things that keep us from recognizing Christ as the Lord of our lives, and of all of history and creation.

Summarize.

Wrap-up. Encourage people to look ahead to next week by taking note how the village people of Galilee received Jesus (6:53-56) and comparing this to the attitudes of the Pharisees and scribes of Jerusalem (7:1-6).

Worship.

MARK 7:1–8:26

A Light to the Gentiles

Jesus continued to widen the scope of His ministry in various ways. He not only healed the sick and cast out demons, but He gave His twelve closest followers authority to do likewise. In addition, He demonstrated His lordship over all of creation by feeding the 5,000 and walking upon the Sea of Galilee. Crowds continued to gather to hear Him preach and receive His healing touch (6:7-13,30-56).

Yet such popular appeal did not translate into widespread faith. Opposition from those of His hometown (6:1-7) and from the religious leaders of Jerusalem (7:5) finally led Jesus to strike out once again into Gentile territory, this time northward to Tyre and Sidon, then south again to Decapolis, where He had healed the demon-possessed man (5:1-20). If His own people would not listen, then Jesus would fulfill the mission foretold by the prophet Isaiah: to be a "light to the Gentiles" (Isaiah 49:6). Read 7:1–8:26.

The evil within (7:1-23)

Unclean (7:2). The Greek word is not one used to designate something dirty or unhygienic, but rather something "common," such as "common people" (as opposed to the Pharisees) or the "common" Greek language used in everyday conversation (as opposed to highly polished literary Greek). It was also used to designate ceremonial uncleanness.

---

1. Note that when Jesus replied to the Pharisees (7:6-13) He did not really answer their question.

_____

_____

_____

_____

_____

_____

For Thought and Discussion: Try to pinpoint some examples in the present-day Church of the sort of traditional "external" religion Jesus condemned (Mark 7:9-19). Which of these, if any, have been a part of your Christian experience?

Optional Application: Consider Jesus' list of things within us that make us unclean (7:21-23). Which are problems for you? How does a person deal with such things? If you don't know, how can you find out?

For Thought and Discussion: The same Jesus who declared all foods clean, thus overturning the Mosaic dietary laws (Mark 7:19), also said that He had come "not to abolish the Law" (Matthew 5:17) and charged the Pharisees with breaking the Law of Moses (Mark 7:9). Discuss how these two views of the Law might be resolved.

Tradition of the elders (7:3,5). The mass of oral tradition formulated by the rabbis in order to apply the Law of Moses to specific situations. About 200 AD it was written down as the Mishnah, but in Jesus' day was still in oral form. This tradition was passed on from generation to generation and was considered by the scribes and Pharisees to be as binding as the Law of Moses itself.

Corban (7:11). One such "tradition of the elders" whereby a man could declare a portion of his wealth to be "dedicated to God." The person who designated his money as Corban did not have to give it to God during his lifetime—a fact that led to the abuse of which Jesus speaks. The origins of both this Aramaic word and the custom to which it refers are uncertain.

2. a. What was Jesus' view of the authority of the Law of Moses (7:10,19)?

_____

_____

_____

_____

_____

   b. In light of this, what authority should Christians ascribe to the Old Testament?

78

_____

_____

_____

_____

_____

3. In your own words, explain the difference between the Pharisees' view of "uncleanness" and Jesus' view (7:14-23).

_____

_____

_____

_____

_____

The faith of a Gentile (7:24-30)

Dogs (7:27). Jesus used the word meaning "little dogs" or "puppies." Such diminutives were often used as terms of affection in Jesus' day. Thus He was probably referring not to the bands of dogs roaming the streets, but to pets who ate leftovers after the family had eaten.

4. Why do you think Jesus spoke as He did to this Gentile woman when she sought healing for her daughter (7:26-27)?

_____

_____

_____

_____

_____

Optional Application:
What was there about
the attitude of the Gen-
tile woman when she
went to Jesus for help
(7:25-28) that you can
apply to your prayer life?

5. What does the woman's reply to Jesus (7:28) tell us about her attitude toward Him?

_____

_____

_____

_____

6. Do you see any connection between Jesus' actions in this section (7:24-30) and His teaching in the previous section (7:1-23)? If so, explain.

_____

_____

_____

_____

_____

Jesus heals a deaf-mute (7:31-37)

7. Jesus could have healed the deaf-mute instantly with a word. Why do you think He took him aside from the crowd and touched the man's ears and tongue?

_____

_____

_____

_____

8. Compare the reaction of the people of Decapolis to this miracle with their reaction to the first miracle Jesus performed in that region (5:1-20). What do you suppose accounted for the difference?

_____

_____

_____

_____

_____

Feeding the 4,000 (8:1-10)

_____

Another large crowd (8:1). Almost certainly Gentiles
(or at least a mixed audience), since this entire
section (7:24–8:10) emphasizes that Jesus did the
same sort of miracles in Gentile territory that He
had done among the Jews. The introductory
words of verse 1, "During those days," tie this
account with the preceding miracles done among
the Gentiles.

_____

9. What does the disciples' response to Jesus (8:4) tell
us about their faith?

_____

_____

_____

Dalmanutha (8:10). The identity of this city or region
is unknown. Matthew 15:39 says Jesus went to
Magadan, which was located on the western shore
of the Sea of Galilee. If Dalmanutha and Magadan
were two places located near each other, Mark is
indicating here that Jesus has now gone back to
Jewish territory. The fact that He again encounters
the Pharisees in the following section (8:11) sup-
ports this theory.

The yeast of the Pharisees (8:11-21)

_____

Sign from heaven (8:11). The Pharisees were not asking for more miracles such as healings or casting
out demons. Rather, they wanted the sort of "sign
from heaven" that would accompany the Son of
man promised in Daniel 7:13. They still looked for

For Thought and Discussion: What sort of things do you think kept the disciples from recognizing who Jesus was? What keeps us from trusting Jesus today?

the messianic Kingdom of God to break into human history in spectacular fashion, as opposed to the hidden "secret" of the Kingdom described by Jesus in His parables (Mark 4).

Yeast (8:15). Yeast, or leaven, was used in baking bread. In rabbinical writings yeast is usually, though not always, a symbol for evil.

10. a. In light of the Pharisees' demand for a sign from heaven (8:11) and their view of the Kingdom of God, to what do you think Jesus refers when He speaks of the "yeast of the Pharisees" (8:15)?

_____

_____

_____

_____

b. Is the yeast of Herod the same as, or different from, the yeast of the Pharisees? If different, what is it?

_____

_____

_____

_____

A second touch (8:22-26)

11. Mark places this story immediately after Jesus twice asks the disciples, "Do you still not understand [who I am]?" (8:17,21).

a. What is unique about this healing as opposed to every other healing recorded by Mark?

_____

_____

_____

b. Do you see a connection between this gradual healing and the disciples' slowness to understand who Jesus is? Explain.

_____

_____

_____

_____

12. Why do you think Jesus healed this man apart from the crowds, then urged him not even to go into the village?

_____

_____

_____

_____

13. What recurring themes about Jesus did you notice in this section (7:1–8:26), and what new truths did you learn?

_____

_____

_____

_____

_____

_____

14. Write down how you hope to apply one old theme or one new truth to your life this week.

_____

_____

_____

_____

For the group

Warm-up. Ask each group member to share one thing which makes it hard for him or her to keep trusting God.

Read aloud and summarize.

Questions. Call attention to the continuing opposition of the Jewish religious leaders to Jesus. Compare their criticism of Jesus in Mark 7:5 with the previous criticism found in 3:22. Note how their objections to what Jesus is doing have descended from the blasphemous (3:29) to the ludicrous and hypocritical (7:5-8).

Ask group members how Jesus' indictment of human nature (7:21-23) makes them feel. Compare Jesus' view of the causes of evil with those we hear in the modern media and from our educational system. If anyone expresses reservations about what Jesus says here, emphasize that believing in Christ includes believing His assessment of what we are.

Talk about how, in practice, we deal with the things from within that make us unclean. Do we ignore them? Pray a lot and hope they go away? Try harder?

Jesus' trip to Tyre and Sidon marks His first extended journey into Gentile territory. Mark uses these geographical points of reference to let his Gentile readers know that the gospel is for them as well as for the Jews, and that the idea of a Gentile mission began with Jesus Himself.

How is it that the "sign from heaven" which the Pharisees sought (8:11) is in fact "yeast," or a pervasive evil influence which tends to permeate all that it touches (8:14)? Did not Jesus do many mighty works? What, then, would be wrong with asking for one more? Try to draw parallels and applications for today.

Conclude by noting Mark's continuing emphasis on how slow the disciples were to recognize who Jesus was. Refer to the "For Thought and Discussion" question on page 82 to guide you here.

Summarize.

Wrap-up. Review what the disciples have learned about Jesus thus far, and what they seem to have missed. The next lesson will show Jesus revealing Himself to the Twelve as never before.

Worship.

MARK 8:27–9:29

The Turning Point

As Jesus ended His tour of Gentile territory, His ministry seemed to have reached a stalemate of sorts. Crowds still flocked to see Him, but more out of curiosity than conviction. To be sure, some of the people, Jews and Gentiles alike, believed in Him. But even His closest followers did not fully understand who He was (and therefore what they believed). Furthermore, opposition from the religious establishment continued, as scribal "truth squads" continued to wend their way north from Jerusalem to harrass Jesus (7:1-5, 8:11-13).

A turning point had come. The time was ripe for Jesus to reveal Himself to His closest followers in no uncertain terms (8:27-30). At the same time, Jesus would continue to hide His messiahship from the crowds, who were not expecting a Messiah who would suffer and die. Indeed, Jesus' own disciples could make no sense of His direct statements about rejection, death, and rising again (8:31-33). Even when He gave them a foretaste of the coming Kingdom (9:1-13), the Twelve could comprehend His mission no better than they were able to understand the parables. Read 8:27–9:29.

Peter's confession (8:27-30)

Caesarea Philippi (8:27). A Roman city located near Dan, the northernmost town of the old Kingdom of Israel. Caesarea Philippi was named after Philip

For Further Study:
Compare Mark's account of Peter's confession with that of Matthew (Matthew 16:13-20). List all the truths you learn from Matthew's account that Mark does not mention.

For Thought and Discussion: Why do you think Jesus revealed Himself as Messiah at Caesarea Philippi, and not in Galilee or Jerusalem?

the tetrarch (Luke 3:1), who rebuilt it following the death of Herod the Great. At the time of Christ this city was a center of Greco-Roman culture, though the population of the surrounding villages included Jews as well as Gentiles (see the reference to "teachers of the law" in Mark 9:14). Thus Caesarea Philippi was a crossroads of sorts between Jewish and Gentile cultures.

1. Why do you think Jesus waited until this point in His ministry to reveal Himself as Messiah?

_____

_____

_____

_____

_____

2. Why do you suppose Jesus warned the Twelve not to tell anyone He was the Messiah (8:30)?

_____

_____

_____

_____

Jesus foretells His death (8:31-33)

Rebuke (8:32,33). The Greek word, one of strong admonishment, is the same word translated "warned" in 8:30.

3. What do "Satan" and the "things of men" have in common that would make Jesus link them together in the same breath?

_____

_____

86

The cost of discipleship (8:34-38)

Take up his cross (8:34). Under Roman law, a criminal condemned to death by crucifixion was required to carry his cross to the execution site, as Jesus was required to do (Luke 23:26).

Soul (8:36). In Jewish thought the "soul" referred not merely to a disembodied consciousness, but to one's entire life. The same Greek word (*psyché*) is translated "life" in Mark 8:35.

4. Mark 8:34 notes that Jesus "called the crowd to him along with his disciples." In light of His message in verses 35-37, what significance do you attach to this?

_____

_____

_____

_____

5. According to Jesus, what sort of attitude and behavior characterizes the person who "wants to save his life" (8:35)? Compare verse 35 with the parallel statements in verses 36 and 38 as you answer this.

_____

_____

_____

_____

6. Keeping in mind the significance of the word "cross" in Jesus' day (see note on 8:34, above), how would you apply Jesus' command to "take up your cross" to your life?

87

_____

_____

_____

_____

_____

_____

The Transfiguration:
the Kingdom come (9:1-13)

The kingdom of God come with power (9:1). Many
scholars see in this saying a reference to the second coming of Christ, and thus conclude that
Jesus believed He would return before some of
His disciples died. Others see it as a reference to
the coming of the Holy Spirit at Pentecost (Acts
2:1-21). It is worth, noting, however, that all three
Synoptic Gospels link this saying with the account
of the Transfiguration of Jesus (compare Matthew
16:28–17:13 and Luke 9:27-36). It is therefore
highly probable that they saw the Transfiguration
as in some sense fulfilling this saying.

Cloud (9:7). In the Old Testament, the cloud is a sign
of God's presence and glory (see e.g., Exodus
16:10, 19:9; Leviticus 16:2).

7. In light of what Jesus had just told the Twelve and
the crowds in Mark 8:31-38, why do you think He
revealed Himself so gloriously just six days later?

_____

_____

_____

8. Elijah and Moses were prominent in first-century
Jewish thought. Moses represented the Law and
Elijah represented the Prophets—the two main

divisions of the Jewish Scriptures. Why would God choose these men to appear with Jesus?

_____

_____

_____

_____

Optional Application: Pray this week for the courage to obey the voice of Jesus only (9:7-8), and not the many other voices in the world which compete for our attention.

9. What is the significance of God's reply to Peter (9:7) and the fact that following the voice from heaven, the disciples saw only Jesus (9:8)?

_____

_____

_____

_____

_____

_____

The coming of Elijah (9:9-13)

10. According to verse 10, what must have been the topic of conversation between Jesus, Elijah and Moses? (Compare Luke 9:31.)

_____

_____

_____

11. a. Reread carefully Mark 9:11-13. Why did the disciples ask Jesus about Elijah?

_____

_____

_____

_____

Optional Application:
How are the words, "I do believe; help me overcome my unbelief!" relevant to your prayer life?

Optional Application:
Apply Mark 9:24 to your prayer life this week by:
   a. Thinking carefully about those areas in your life where you do trust God, and those areas where you still feel plagued by unbelief;
   b. Praying specifically to the Lord that He might help you overcome those areas of unbelief (concentrate on just a few).

b. About whom was Jesus speaking when He said "Elijah has come"?

_____

Jesus heals a demon-possessed boy (9:14-29)

12. According to Jesus, why were the disciples unable to cast the demon out of the boy (9:19,29)?

_____

_____

_____

_____

_____

13. How do you think prayer and faith are related to each other?

_____

_____

_____

_____

_____

14. Summarize how Mark depicts the faith of the disciples in this entire section (8:27–9:29).

_____

_____

_____

_____

90

15. List any questions you have about this section.

_____

_____

_____

_____

For the group

Warm-up. Have each group member briefly answer the question, "What is faith?"

Read aloud and summarize.

Questions. Even as Peter finally recognized Jesus to be the Messiah (8:29), he still could not bring himself to believe in a *suffering* Messiah (8:32). Peter had his agenda in life, and following a suffering Messiah was not part of it! At this point you may wish to ask group members "What is there on your agenda that keeps you from following Christ?" (Be willing to take the lead!) You may wish to use the "Optional Application" on page 89 to help you.

Faith and unbelief are major themes of this lesson. Draw attention to how Mark 8:27–9:29 records instances of each, then ask group members to apply these lessons of faith and warnings about unbelief to their lives.

Compare the Kingdom and messiahship offered by Jesus with those anticipated and desired by His followers. Pose the following question: "In what ways do people today—including professing Christians—try to redefine Jesus' Kingdom and messiahship in order to suit their desires?"

If Mark's audience was indeed Roman Christians suffering under persecution, how would the account of the Transfiguration encourage them? What encouragement does it give to you?

The last word of this portion of Mark's Gospel is "prayer." Jesus' disciples may have taken for granted the authority given them by Jesus earlier to cast out demons (Mark 6:7-13), thinking that they now possessed some inherent power to do such great works. What they needed to learn was moment-by-moment

91

dependence upon God—and prayer is the supreme expression of such dependence.

If you do nothing else in studying lesson 9, be sure to emphasize the importance of systematic prayer both in Jesus' life and the life of the Christian. Refer in particular to the last two "Optional Application" questions.

Summarize.

Wrap-up. Ask group members to spend time this coming week listing ways in which the study group can become more effective in praying for one another's needs. Be prepared to share these next time.

Worship.

MARK 9:30–10:12

En Route to Jerusalem

Jesus had finally revealed to the Twelve that He was the Christ (8:27-30). Yet even after this revelation, they could not comprehend what His mission was about. A glimpse of the King's future glory, intended to reassure His three closest followers of the triumph that would follow His suffering, instead produced nothing but confusion (9:2-13). And the rest of the Twelve did not even have enough faith to minister in Jesus' name, despite having been given the authority to do so earlier (9:14-29; see 6:7-13).

His public ministry now largely behind Him, the stage was set for Jesus' final trip to Jerusalem. Behind Him followed a band of bewildered disciples (9:32); ahead lay His destiny. Only when this final act of the drama was played out would His followers begin to realize the meaning of His ministry on earth. But until that time, He still had much to teach them about what it meant to be a citizen of the Kingdom of God.

Jesus foretells His death a second time (9:30-32)

Be betrayed (9:31). The Greek verb here may be translated one of three ways: "be betrayed," "be delivered over to," or "deliver himself over to." In the first instance Judas would be the implied subject, while in the second the subject could be either Judas or God. In the third instance Jesus Himself would be the subject, thus emphasizing His control over His own destiny.

Optional Application:
Pray that God will show
you one specific way
that you can serve one
specific person this
week.

1. Why do you think the disciples were afraid to ask
   Jesus about what He meant when He spoke of
   being killed and rising again?

   _____

   _____

   _____

   _____

   _____

Who is the greatest? (9:33-50)

2. What events prior to their argument (9:33-34)
   might have prompted the Twelve to quarrel over
   which of them was "the greatest"?

   _____

   _____

   _____

   _____

3. What does this argument tell us about their understanding of who Jesus was and why He came?

   _____

   _____

   _____

   _____

Servant (9:35). The Greek word means not a hired
   hand, but rather those who serve a king (see
   Matthew 22:13). The same word is used when
   Paul speaks of "deacons" (1 Timothy 3:8) or "min-
   isters" (2 Corinthians 3:6).

4. Jesus defined greatness in terms of being a servant.

a. Why do you think Jesus used a child to illustrate His point (9:36-37)?

_____

_____

_____

_____

Optional Application: Jesus said, "Whoever is not against us is for us" (Mark 9:40). How can we apply this truth to our lives in light of the present-day reality of numerous Christian denominations?

b. What does it mean to minister/serve "in Jesus' name" (9:37,38-39,41)? Try to give some concrete examples.

_____

_____

_____

_____

_____

5. Jesus told the Twelve, "Whoever is not against us is for us" (9:40).

a. Why do you think the Twelve tried to prevent someone who wasn't part of their group from casting out demons using Jesus' name?

_____

_____

_____

_____

_____

b. What application do you see in this episode for Christians today?

_____

_____

_____

_____

_____

6. What connection do you see between the "one-up-manship" of the Twelve (9:33-34,38) and the danger of causing believers in Jesus to sin (9:42)?

_____

_____

_____

_____

_____

Hell (9:43). The word translated "hell" is *gehenna*, a Greek form of the Hebrew *ge hinnom* ("Valley of Hinnom"). This valley, located south of Jerusalem, was used for burning the city's garbage. The fires of Hinnom never went out, and thus came to be used as a symbol for the place of divine punishment. See Isaiah 66:24.

7. Why does Jesus use such radical language (9:43-48) as He urges His followers to avoid sin?

_____

_____

_____

_____

_____

Salt (9:49-50). Salt was always included in Old Testament grain sacrifices (Leviticus 2:13) because it represented purification (salt was commonly used to keep meat from spoiling). It then came to symbolize both the covenant relationship God had with Israel and close fellowship between friends. In the early Church the Lord's Supper was sometimes celebrated with bread and salt, and the expression "to share in the salt" became a technical term for "to celebrate the Lord's Supper."[1]

8. Referring to the previous note on salt, write out a paraphrase of Mark 9:50. Pay attention to the overall context (9:33-50).

_____

_____

_____

_____

9. How should we act so as not to lose our "saltiness" (9:50)?

_____

_____

_____

_____

_____

The question of divorce (10:1-12)

Across the Jordan (10:1). The region of Perea, which was ruled by Herod Antipas. The fact that the Pharisees raised the question of divorce within the domain of Antipas, who had flouted the Old Testament laws of divorce (Mark 6:17-18), may indicate that their question was less a sincere seeking for insight than an attempt to get Jesus in trouble with the local authorities (remember what happened to John the Baptist!).

Certificate of divorce (10:4). A reference to Deuteronomy 24:1, which reads in part: "If a man marries a woman who becomes displeasing to him because he finds something indecent about her, and he writes her a certificate of divorce. . . ." The Jews allowed for divorce; disagreements arose among

For Thought and Discussion: What is the specific "sin" to which Jesus refers in Mark 9:42-50 which merits the fires of hell? Support your answer with evidence from the near context (9:33-50).

For Thought and Discussion: If "salt is good" (9:50), to what sort of "fire" does Jesus refer (9:49) when He assures His disciples that all those who follow Him will be "salted with fire": (a) The "fire" of the Holy Spirit or (b) the "fire" of persecution? Keep in mind both the context of Jesus' remarks within Mark's narrative and the probable circumstances of Mark's readers.

For Thought and Discussion: Explain how Jesus' three groups of statements in Mark 9:35-50 (verses 35-37, 38-42,43-50) relate to the apostles' argument about who was the greatest (9:34).

For Further Study:
Compare Mark 10:1-12
with Deuteronomy
24:1-4, Matthew
19:1-12, Luke 16:18,
and 1 Corinthians
7:10-15. Write out
everything these verses
teach about divorce and
remarriage.

**For Thought and
Discussion:** Read
Deuteronomy 24:1-4. In
light of Jesus' high view
of the Law of Moses on
the one hand (e.g.,
Matthew 5:17-20) and
His strict words concern-
ing divorce and remar-
riage on the other (Mark
10:12), do you regard
His statements in Mark
10:12 as absolute prohi-
bitions? Why or why not?

Optional Application:
If you know a couple
contemplating divorce,
pray for them and ask
the Lord if He might use
you to strengthen their
relationship. (Do this as
an individual; do not
mention this in the study
session unless everyone
in the group is already
aware of the couple's
situation.)

the rabbis as to what constituted "indecent"
behavior, however. The school of one rabbi (Rabbi
Shammai) understood these words to refer to
moral indecency—i.e., adultery. While the followers of another (Rabbi Hillel) viewed "indecency" so
broadly that it could even include the wife's burning her husband's breakfast!

10. When Jesus asked the Pharisees "What did Moses
command you?" (10:3), they responded "Moses
permitted" (10:4). What is the significance of this
difference?

_____

_____

_____

_____

11. What does Jesus' reply to the Pharisees' question
("Is it lawful?"—10:2) tell us about His view of the
relationship between Law on the one hand and the
will of God on the other (10:5-9)?

_____

_____

_____

If she divorces her husband (10:12). Jesus recognized
the legal right of a woman to divorce her husband,
a right not recognized in Judaism.

12. What does Jesus prohibit in Mark 10:12, and what
does He not prohibit?

_____

_____

_____

98

13. In your own words, summarize Jesus' view of marriage.

_____

_____

_____

_____

_____

14. What key truths stand out to you from 9:30–10:12?

_____

_____

_____

_____

15. List any questions you have about this section.

_____

_____

_____

_____

For the group

Warm-up. Ask each group member to recall one person he or she thought of as being "great" while growing up, and to share why he or she regarded that person as "great."

Read aloud and summarize.

Questions. Emphasize how the different incidents in Mark 9:33-50 revolve around one theme: what it means to be "great" in the Kingdom of God. Ask group members to pick out key words or phrases that illustrate this theme, and talk about their meaning. Then ponder what incidents prior to Mark 9:33 might have caused the argument mentioned in 9:34 (see question

2). Finally, encourage participants to discuss what sorts of things cause such dissension among Christians today, and how to overcome these divisions and have "peace with one another" (Mark 9:50).

Be very sensitive to every person in the group when discussing Mark 10:1-12. Point out that Jesus' teaching on divorce was meant not so much to pass judgment on individuals as it was to affirm the sanctity of marriage and to protect women from being cast off at a husband's whim. (Contrast this with the liberal attitude toward divorce exemplified by the Pharisees, who cared less about the sanctity of marriage than they did about justifying themselves.)

Summarize.

Wrap-up. Have group members briefly share their ideas as to how the group might more effectively pray for one another's needs (see "Wrap-up" for lesson 9, page 91). Then pray that God will give you (1) increasing insight as to how radically the values of the Kingdom of God differ from the values of the society in which we live and (2) wisdom to live out those "Kingdom values" in our society.

Worship.

1. Oscar Cullmann, *Essays on the Lord's Supper* (Philadelphia: John Knox Press, 1958), page 12.

MARK 10:13-52

The Servant Messiah

As Jesus continued on toward Jerusalem, His teaching took on an increasingly urgent note. Those who would follow Him, Jesus insisted, must not think that citizenship in God's Kingdom would confer upon them worldly greatness. To the contrary, they could look forward to persecution, for their way of life as followers of Jesus would run counter to the prevailing wisdom of the day. Yet such must be their lot if they wished to escape God's judgment (Mark 9:33-50).

Jesus went on to amaze His disciples still further (10:24,26) by holding up little children, rather than persons of status and wealth, as examples of true citizens of the Kingdom of God (10:13-31). Even more important, He finally revealed to His followers the full meaning of His messiahship (10:45). Having done that, He was prepared to enter Jerusalem to accomplish that which He came to do.

Optional Application: Think of one way in which you need to become more like the "little child" of whom Jesus spoke (10:15), and pray this week that God will work that change in your life.

Receive the Kingdom as a child
(Mark 10:13-16)

1. How can we apply Jesus' attitude toward little children to . . .

our attitude toward God?

_____

_____

_____

our regard for children?

_____

_____

_____

_____

Riches an obstacle to the Kingdom
(Mark 10:17-31)

2. Describe the attitude of the wealthy man as he came to Jesus.

_____

_____

_____

_____

3. In Mark 10:18 Jesus responds to the man: "Why do you call me good? No one is good—except God alone." Why do you think Jesus said this?

_____

_____

_____

_____

_____

4. Why would selling all of his *earthly* possessions and giving to the poor ensure the wealthy man of "treasure in *heaven*" (Mark 10:21-22; see also Matthew 6:19-21, Luke 12:32-34)?

_____

_____

_____

The rich (10:23). In New Testament times, "to be wealthy was sure evidence of having the blessing of God."[1]

5. Why were Jesus' disciples "amazed" (10:24) at His statement that it was hard for the rich to enter God's Kingdom?

_____

_____

_____

_____

The eye of a needle (10:25). Some interpreters identify the "eye of the needle" with a low, narrow gate leading into Jerusalem at which camels had to kneel in order to get through. But the existence of such a gate has never been established, and Mark 10:26-27 indicates that both Jesus and His disciples understood Him to be talking about spiritual impossibilities, not merely difficulties.

6. a. In Mark 10:27 does Jesus mean that it is humanly impossible (1) for the rich to be saved, or (2) for *anyone*—rich or poor—to be saved? Defend your choice with evidence from the text.

_____

_____

_____

_____

b. What are the implications for us?

_____

_____

_____

_____

For Further Study: Compare the wealthy young man (10:17-22) to Zacchaeus the tax collector (Luke 19:2-10). Why do you think Jesus did not also command Zacchaeus to sell all he had?

For Thought and Discussion: Do you believe Jesus is teaching that only those without wealth can enter the Kingdom of God? Why or why not?

Optional Application: What practical steps can you begin to take this week to insure that you will have "treasure in heaven"?

103

For Thought and Discussion: Compare the values of the Kingdom of God (10:13-45) with those of our present-day society.

7. a. Why did Peter respond to Jesus as he did in 10:28?

_____

_____

_____

_____

b. Why did Jesus answer Peter as He did in 10:29-30?

_____

_____

_____

_____

Jesus foretells His death a third time
(10:32-34)

8. a. When Jesus predicts His death and resurrection this third time, what does He say that He did not say the first two times (8:31, 9:31)?

_____

_____

b. Why do you think He added this?

_____

_____

_____

The Servant Messiah (10:35-45)

9. What are the "baptism" and "cup" of which Jesus speaks (10:38-39)?

_____

_____

10. Contrast Jesus' view of Kingdom citizenship (10:41-44) with that of James and John (10:37).

_____

_____

_____

_____

_____

For Further Study: Compare Mark's reference to Jesus as a "ransom for many" with the following texts: Isaiah 53:5-6; Romans 5:6-8,15-19; 1 Corinthians 15:3; 2 Corinthians 5:21; Hebrews 9:15.

For Thought and Discussion: Read Mark 10:44 in light of 10:35. What limits are there on being a "slave of all"?

For Thought and Discussion: What does the persistence of Bartimaeus (10:48) teach us about prayer?

Ransom for many (10:45). The Greek word translated "ransom" often referred to the price paid to liberate a slave, while the word rendered "for" was used as a term of exchange in the marketplace—including the slave market.

11. In your own words, tell why Jesus came (10:45).

_____

_____

_____

_____

_____

Jesus heals blind Bartimaeus (10:46-52)

Son of David (10:47). The Jews of Jesus' day believed that the Messiah would come from David's kingly line. Many held that this Messiah would be, like David, a warrior-king who would overthrow the occupying forces of Rome and liberate the nation of Israel.

12. This is the only miracle Mark records during Jesus' trip to Jerusalem. Why do you think Jesus singled

105

out Bartimaeus, among the many needy people He must have encountered along the way, for healing?

For Thought and Discussion: During the journey to Jerusalem (9:30–10:52) Mark emphasizes the teachings of Jesus to His disciples, with only one miracle mentioned (the healing of Bartimaeus). What significance do you see in this?

Optional Application: Write down, as recorded in Mark 10:13-45: (a) the requirements of discipleship, and (b) the promises of Jesus to those who follow Him. As you pray during the coming week, allow these promises to motivate you toward following Jesus more closely.

13. Write down what you believe is the single most important truth you learned in this lesson.

14. How is this truth relevant to your life?

15. List any questions you have about this section.

For the group

Warm-up. Ask group members to describe something they still own that is a memento of their childhood.

Read aloud and summarize.

Questions. Give group members a chance to talk about how they might apply Jesus' startling command to the wealthy young man (10:21) to their own lives. Encourage differences of opinion on this one!

Ask participants how they would apply Mark 10:45 to their lives. Then read the following quote from the late Scottish theologian P. T. Forsyth:

> "Christ came not to be ministered to, but to minister; and our first duty, therefore, is to be ministered to by him. First faith, then works."

Did anyone apply Mark 10:45 in the same way Forsyth did? Encourage participants to respond to Forsyth's statement.

Summarize.

Wrap-up. Encourage group members to apply the final "Optional Application" of this lesson ("requirements of discipleship/promises of Jesus") to their lives this coming week.

Worship.

1. Wessel, *Mark*, page 716.

MARK 11:1-33

The Final Week Begins

The gospel of the Kingdom of God was beginning to look like anything but "good news" to the Twelve! Instead of a conquering king, a suffering servant was calling them to a discipleship which bid them not to be served, but to serve (10:41-45). This notion of a Messiah who would suffer for the sins of His people was completely foreign to anything they had been taught.[1]

Jesus had now revealed the full truth about His calling. As He neared Jerusalem, little remained for Him to say. It was time for action.

The triumphal entry into Jerusalem
(Mark 11:1-11)

Bethphage and Bethany (11:1). The precise location of Bethphage is not known. Bethany, located on the eastern slope of the Mount of Olives about two miles from Jerusalem (see John 11:18), was the home village of Jesus' friends Mary, Martha, and Lazarus (John 11:1), and may have served as a sort of "home away from home" for the itinerant Rabbi. According to Matthew 21:1, however, it was Bethphage not Bethany where the disciples found the colt tied up.

Colt . . . which no one has ever ridden (11:2). The colt was that of a donkey (Matthew 21:2, John 12:15). Animals that had never been ridden were regarded as especially suitable for sacred purposes (compare 1 Samuel 6:7).

For Thought and Discussion: The Jews so wanted a conquering Messiah (Mark 11:10) that they did not recognize precisely why Jesus came (10:45). What sort of desires and expectations do you have of God that may cause you not to recognize Jesus when He comes to you?

1. Read Zechariah 9:9. What was Jesus telling the crowds about His Kingdom when He chose to ride a donkey into Jerusalem instead of a war-horse?

_____

_____

_____

Spread their cloaks. . . spread branches (11:8). These were acts of royal homage (see 2 Kings 9:13).[2]

Hosanna! (11:9). The Hebrew word literally means "Save now!" It was an acclamation from Psalm 118:25, which was supposed to be the Psalm sung when the Messiah arrived. Likewise, *Blessed is he who comes in the name of the Lord* quoted Psalm 118:26.

2. What does the reaction of the crowd (11:9-10) tell you about how *they* interpreted Jesus' entry into Jerusalem?

_____

_____

_____

Temple (11:11). Includes the area immediately surrounding the Temple, as well as the Temple building itself. The Jews regarded the Jerusalem Temple and the Law of Moses as the most important religious institutions of their day. The Temple symbolized the glory of God in their midst.

Jesus curses the fig tree (11:12-14,20-25)

Fig tree (11:12). In the Old Testament, the fig tree was sometimes used to represent Israel (Hosea 9:10, Nahum 3:12).

Because it was not the season for figs (11:13). Fig trees around Jerusalem usually leaf out in March or April (and thus look mature from a distance), but they do not produce figs until June.[3] The incident recorded in Mark 11:12-14 took place just before Passover, in either March or April.

3. Write down your initial reaction to the cursing of the fig tree. How does it differ from every other miracle Jesus performed?

_____

_____

_____

4. Some commentators see the cursing of the fig tree as an acted-out parable. If this is the case, and if the fig tree represents Israel, what point was Jesus trying to make? (Note how the cleansing of the Temple is sandwiched in between the two halves of the fig-tree account.)

_____

_____

_____

_____

5. Jesus also used the fig-tree incident as an object-lesson for prayer (11:20-25). List the elements Jesus singles out here for a strong prayer life.

_____

_____

_____

6. What do you make of 11:22-25? How is it relevant to your own experience of prayer?

_____

_____

_____

Optional Application: Jesus cursed a fig tree which looked beautiful from a distance but bore no fruit. Ask God to show you one specific area of your life which may appear spiritually mature at first glance, but where you have yet to bear significant fruit. Then, pray for growth in that area.

Optional Application: As you pray this week, ask God to reveal to you if there is anyone against whom you still hold a grudge. Then apply 11:25.

For Further Study: Compare Jesus' teachings on prayer and forgiveness in Mark 11:22-25 with those in Matthew 6:9-15 and Luke 11:2-4.

For Further Study: How do John 15:7 and James 4:3 further clarify Jesus' promises of answered prayer?

For Thought and Discussion: a. What is the relationship between faith in God and forgiving others?

b. Why do you think Jesus ties together God's forgiveness of us and our forgiving others?

The cleansing of the Temple (11:15-19)

Buying and selling (11:15). Jewish pilgrims from throughout the Roman Empire came to Jerusalem for the Passover. Since it was impossible for many of them to bring the animals necessary for the temple sacrifices, such animals—cattle, lambs, and birds—were sold in the "Court of the Gentiles," an area just outside the Temple that Gentiles could enter, but beyond which they could not go. This area was supposed to be a place where Gentiles could come and encounter the true God (1 Kings 8:41-43).

Money changers (11:15). The Roman money the pilgrims brought to Jerusalem had to be changed into the local currency with which the annual temple tax was paid. The money changers were not above making a profit on such transactions.

Both the sale of animals for sacrifice and the moneychanging activities were authorized by the high priest, and the chief priestly families probably owned a sizable piece of the action.

7. a. Whose authority was Jesus challenging when He drove the moneychangers from the Temple area?

b. What therefore was He saying about His own authority?

8. What do both the cursing of the fig tree and the cleansing of the Temple tell us about Jesus' attitude toward the spiritual condition of the people of Israel?

112

_____

_____

_____

_____

9. Read Mark 11:17 in light of Isaiah 56:6-7. Why was Jesus so upset at the marketplace atmosphere in the "Court of the Gentiles"?

_____

_____

_____

_____

"By what authority?" (11:27-33)

From heaven (11:30). The Jews commonly substituted the word "heaven" for "God," out of respect for the Divine Name.

10. What are "these things" to which the religious leaders of Jerusalem refer in 11:28?

_____

_____

11. Why do you think Jesus did not answer the religious leaders directly, but instead posed a question in response to their question?

_____

_____

_____

12. What have Jesus' actions in 11:1-33 demonstrated about His view of Himself and His mission?

_____

_____

Optional Application: What sort of practices in the Church today hinder nonChristians from coming to know Christ?

For Further Study: For further insight into John the Baptist's relationship with the religious leaders on the one hand, and his popularity with the people on the other, read Matthew 3:1-12.

Optional Application: Make a list of modern-day "authorities" who influence public opinion (for example: the media, politicians, and even religious leaders). Briefly note how their values differ from the values of the Kingdom of God, and ask God to give you strength and insight to follow His authority, not that of the world.

_____

_____

_____

13. Write down any questions you have about this chapter.

_____

_____

_____

_____

For the group

Warm-up. Briefly describe a time when you felt God wasn't answering your prayers. Don't worry so much about sharing the details of the situation as about telling how you felt in the situation.

Read aloud and summarize.

Questions. Point out that the Jews expected their coming Messiah, the "Son of David," to judge the Gentiles and vindicate Israel. By way of contrast, Jesus' first actions following His entry into Jerusalem involved judging *Jewish* religious practices. Do you see any applications for the Church today?

Jesus' statements about faith and prayer (11:22-25) raise the question of why God at times appears *not* to answer our prayers. Allow group members to share honestly any frustrations or doubts they have about prayer. Talk about why it often seems that God isn't answering even when we believe He is able to do what we're asking. Try to avoid pat answers.

Summarize.

Wrap-up. In this and the following lesson, Jesus calls into question many of the most cherished beliefs of His day. Encourage group members to ask themselves as they study, "What might Jesus be calling into question

114

in *my* life? How ought I to respond?" Follow up on this in next week's lesson.

Worship. Thank God that He is sovereign, and that He knows that our *needs* are not always the same as our desires.

1. Oscar Cullmann, *The Christology of the New Testament.* (Philadelphia, PA: Westminster, 1959), page 56.
2. Wessel, *Mark,* page 724.
3. Wessel, *Mark,* page 726.

MARK 12:1-44

Jesus Confronts the Religious Leaders

When Jesus entered Jerusalem as Israel's Messiah, He immediately turned the messianic expectations of official Judaism upside down. Instead of coming as a conquering king, He came as a "gentle" Messiah, riding on a donkey. Then His first act of judgment was not against the Gentiles, but against the religious practices taking place within the Temple itself.

When challenged by the religious leaders, Jesus immediately took the offensive (11:27–12:12). Even as He spoke in parables, His message was now clear to all: He had come not to judge the Gentiles and justify Israel, but rather to judge Israel for her hypocritical worship and to call all people to a true obedience based not on love of wealth and power (12:38-40), but on love of God and neighbor (12:28-34).

Parable of the vineyard (12:1-12)

Vineyard (12:1). Jesus' words here reflect the language of Isaiah 5:1-2, where the prophet likens Israel to a vineyard.

1. a. To whom is Jesus speaking in 12:1? Whom do the "farmers" of 12:1 represent?

_____

b. Whom do the "servants" of verses 2 through 5 represent?

_____

c. Who is the "son" of verse 6?

_____

d. Who are the "others" of verse 9?

_____

e. Write down the meaning of the entire parable.

_____

_____

_____

Stone . . . capstone (12:10). Jesus quotes Psalm 118:22-23 (the same messianic psalm quoted when He entered Jerusalem). In the original context the rejected stone was Israel, once shamed in exile but later returned from exile to the status of nationhood (see Psalm 118:1-3).

2. Read Mark 12:10-11. What is the significance of Jesus saying He will fulfill Psalm 118:22-23?

_____

_____

_____

_____

God and Caesar (12:13-17)

Pharisees and Herodians (12:13). See the note on Mark 3:1-6. The Herodians had no objections to paying taxes (actually a political tribute) to Rome, while the Pharisees disliked the Roman tax but did not actively oppose it. The Pharisees' more activist counterparts, the Zealots (see note on Mark 3:18), refused to pay the tax, seeing in such payment an admission that Rome had the right to rule Palestine.

3. Specifically what do you think the Pharisees and Herodians were trying to accomplish when they asked Jesus if one should pay taxes to Caesar?

_____

_____

_____

_____

Denarius . . . coin (12:15-16). It appears Jesus' questioners had such a coin readily at hand. "This implies that they had already answered their own question. It was Caesar's coinage they were using (v. 16); and by using it they were tacitly acknowledging Caesar's authority and thus their obligation to pay the tax."[1]

4. Jesus gave His questioners an ambiguous answer. How do you interpret what He said?

_____

_____

_____

_____

_____

The God of the living (12:18-27)

Sadducees (12:18). One of the four major Jewish sects of New Testament times, the other three being the Pharisees, Zealots, and Essenes. The Sadducees represented the property-owning urban class and were mainly centered in Jerusalem. They were numerically small but of great political influence due to their wealth, though not particularly popular with the people. When Jerusalem was destroyed in AD 70 they disappeared from history.

   The Sadducees denied the doctrine of the resurrection of the body because they held only the

For Thought and Discussion: If we can recognize a coin that belongs to Caesar by the fact that it bears his image, how can we recognize what belongs to God? How is this relevant to Jesus' response in 12:17?

For Further Study: Jesus' response to the question about paying taxes to Caesar (12:13-17) presupposes a particular view of the relationship between the Christian and the State. Examine New Testament teachings concerning the State in Acts 5:29, Romans 13:1-7, 1 Timothy 2:1-4, 1 Peter 2:13-17, and Revelation 13:1-10.

Optional Application: As citizens of a pluralistic democracy, how should we apply Jesus' instruction to "Give to Caesar what is Caesar's and to God what is God's"?

119

Optional Application:
Pray this week that God
would reveal to you any
areas of your life in
which you lack faith in
either the Scriptures or
God's power. Then ask
for courage to trust God
in these matters.

five books of Moses (Genesis through Deuteronomy) to be sacred Scripture, and they did not find
any clear teaching of such a resurrection in those
five books.

Moses wrote . . . (12:19). See Deuteronomy 25:5-6.
The purpose of this law was to protect the widow
and guarantee the continuance of the family line.

Seven brothers . . . (12:20). This absurd little story
may have been a standing joke the Sadducees used
to embarrass their more popular rivals, the Pharisees, who did believe in the resurrection (see Acts
23:8).

Angels (12:25). The Sadducees also denied the
existence of angels.

5. According to Jesus (12:24), the Sadducees did "not
know" two things. Explain how Jesus responded to
each of these two points of Sadduceean ignorance.

a. Ignorance about the Scriptures.

_____

_____

_____

_____

b. Ignorance about the power of God.

_____

_____

_____

_____

The great commandment (12:28-34)

Hear, O Israel . . . (12:29). This Old Testament text
was the first verse of a Hebrew liturgy known as
the *Shema* (Hebrew for "Hear!"), which included
Deuteronomy 6:4-9 and 11:13-21.

6. What does the conversation between Jesus and the teacher of the Law tell us about the relationship between the Old Testament Law and the gospel of Christ?

_____

_____

_____

_____

_____

Son of David (12:35-37)

Son (12:37). Standard Jewish belief held that no son could be greater than his father.

_____

7. Summarize the point Jesus was trying to make when He quoted Psalm 110:1.

_____

_____

_____

_____

_____

Beware! (12:38-40)

Devour widows' houses (12:40). "Since the teachers of the law were not allowed to be paid for their services, they were dependent on the gifts of patrons for their livelihood. Such a system was vulnerable to abuses. Wealthy widows especially were preyed on by the greedy and unscrupulous among these men."[2]

8. a. Many people think the really big sins are things like sexual promiscuity or drug use. What really big sins does Jesus point out in 12:38-40?

For Thought and Discussion: Do you think the large crowd listened to Jesus "with delight" (12:37) because (a) they admired what He was saying, or (b) they enjoyed seeing Jesus stump the "theologians"? Why do you think that?

For Further Study: Read Matthew 6:19-24; Luke 12:15-21, 16:19-31; 1 Timothy 6:7-10. Why do New Testament writers take such pains to warn us about accumulating wealth?

121

For Thought and Discussion: What made the poor widow's tiny contribution to the Temple treasury greater in Jesus' eyes than the large sums of money given by the wealthy (12:41-44)?

Optional Application: a. What emotions arise in you when you think about giving to God sacrificially?
b. Talk with God about how you should use the wealth He has given you.

_____

_____

_____

_____

_____

b. Why are these sins so serious?

_____

_____

_____

_____

The widow's offering (12:41-44)

Copper coins (12:42). Greek *lepta*, the plural of *lepton*. The lepton was the smallest coin in circulation in Palestine, worth one sixty-fourth of a denarius (the daily wage of a hired worker; see note on Mark 6:37).

Fraction of a penny (12:42). In the *New International Version* these four words translate the single Greek word *kodrantes*, which is a transliteration of the Latin *quadrans*, a Roman copper coin worth the same as a lepton. The fact that Mark explains the value of the Palestinian lepton by comparing it to the quadrans, a coin known only in the western portion of the Roman empire, strongly suggests that he was writing to Romans.

9. What was so significant about the poor widow's offering that Jesus went out of His way to call His disciples and tell them about it (12:43)?

_____

_____

_____

10. Review Mark 12. How would you summarize the basic problem that was corrupting the religious system of first-century Jerusalem?

_____

_____

_____

_____

_____

11. What's your impression of Jesus in this chapter? What do you observe about His personality and abilities?

_____

_____

_____

_____

12. List any questions you have about this chapter.

_____

_____

_____

_____

_____

For the group

Warm-up. The "wrap-up" question of lesson 12 was: "What might Jesus be calling into question in *my* life?" Ask participants if they have thought about this question during the past week. How has Jesus been disrupting your assumptions about life?

Read aloud and summarize.

Questions. Draw attention to how Jesus deals with the various groups of religious leaders (Pharisees, Sadducees, Herodians, teachers of the Law). What were some of their attitudes and practices that Jesus opposed? Which of these are still present today, even within the Church itself, and how ought we to respond?

In this entire chapter, Jesus has only two words of commendation (12:34,43-44). Encourage group members to discuss what these two very different people—one a member of the religious establishment, the other an outsider—had in common that caused Jesus to commend them both.

If the question of how we as Christians ought to use our accumulated wealth does not arise spontaneously during the group's discussion, be sure to bring it up. What is the relationship between true faith and the compassionate use of wealth?

Summarize.

Wrap-up. Next week's lesson centers on the second coming of Christ. Urge group members to ask themselves, as they study lesson 14, "Does the fact that Jesus is coming again make any practical difference in my Christian life?"

Worship. Thank God for His many gifts, and pray for wisdom as to how you might use them to glorify Christ.

1. Wessel, *Mark*, page 734.
2. Wessel, *Mark*, page 740.

MARK 13:1-37

The Second Coming of Christ

Jesus entered Jerusalem, not to deliver Israel from the Roman occupation, but to pronounce judgment upon her infidelities. The Temple, a symbol of God's presence with His people, received not a blessing but a purging from its Lord. And as He taught the crowds and challenged the religious leaders, Jesus called into question virtually every religious institution and practice of God's chosen nation.

Yet even after witnessing all of this, His disciples failed to comprehend the full impact of His words. Their minds were still conformed to the present age; thus, as they left the Temple (13:1) they remarked on its glorious buildings. Jesus, however, was looking to the future. The glory of the Lord would appear only when the glory of human pride was completely cast down. Read Mark 13:1-37.

The beginning of the end (13:1-8)

Magnificent buildings (13:1). Herod the Great built the Jerusalem Temple of Jesus' time. It was much larger than the Temple the Jews built after returning from exile in Babylon in 538 BC, though not as large as Solomon's Temple, which the Babylonians destroyed. Herod rebuilt the post-exilic Temple, which had fallen into disrepair, in order to curry favor with the Jews, who despised Herod as the Roman emperor's today. The Jews were only too happy to have a magnificent Temple once again, but their opinion of Herod did not change.

For Further Study: Compare Mark 13 with Matthew 24 and Luke 21:5-36. Determine how they agree and how they differ.

For Thought and Discussion: Is there anything Christians can do to hasten the second coming of Christ? If so, what is it? If not, why not?

Optional Application: For the next thirty days, pray specifically for (a) a missionary who is taking the gospel to another culture or (b) a Christian being persecuted for his or her faith.

1. a. What was Jesus' primary reason for telling His disciples what signs would precede the end of the age (13:5)?

_____

_____

b. Why do you suppose this was so important?

_____

_____

_____

2. Why did Jesus tell His disciples not to be alarmed when they hear of "wars and rumors of wars" (13:7)?

_____

_____

Birth pains (13:8). This expression probably stems from such Old Testament passages at Isaiah 13:8, 26:17; Jeremiah 4:31, 6:24; and Micah 4:9-10. In Jesus' day the rabbis spoke of "the birth pangs of the Messiah," the period of tribulation immediately preceding the Messianic Age.[1]

The fate of the disciples (13:9-13)

Nations (13:10). Not political nation-states, but rather communities of people who share common cultural, language, and ethnic bonds (Greek *ethnos*).

3. a. What one thing *must* be accomplished prior to the second coming of Christ (13:10)?

_____

_____

126

b. What significance does this have for the Church today?

_____

_____

_____

4. Why do you think Jesus told His followers not to worry about what they should say whenever they were arrested for their faith (13:11)?

_____

_____

_____

_____

5. a. According to Jesus, what must His followers do in order to be assured of eternal life (13:12-13)?

_____

b. Why was this essential?

_____

_____

_____

For Thought and Discussion: Jesus said, "He who stands firm to the end will be saved" (13:13). What does this tell us about the meaning of true Christian faith?

Great tribulation (13:14-23)

Abomination that causes desolation (13:14). This phrase is taken from the book of Daniel, where it occurs four times (8:13, 9:27, 11:31, 12:11). Daniel 11:31 clearly refers to the desecration of the Temple in Jerusalem by Antiochus Epiphanes (168 BC), the Syrian despot who erected an altar to Zeus over the altar of burnt offering, sacrificed a swine on it, and made the practice of Judaism a capital offense. The other three references are not so easy to interpret, though two (9:27, 12:11) appear to refer to the end times. New Testament scholars are divided as to whether Mark 13:14 refers to events preceding the fall of Jerusalem in AD 70, or to events preceding the end of the age just prior to Christ's return. Perhaps it is best to see Jesus as using this phrase in an ambiguous way, thus making possible a double fulfillment: the armies of Rome (AD 70) and the Antichrist (the end of the age).

Flee to the mountains (13:14). "There is a reasonably good tradition that Christians abandoned the city, perhaps in AD 68, about halfway through the siege [of Jerusalem by the armies of Rome]."[2]

6. What portions of this passage indicate that Jesus is talking about the "end times," and not merely the fall of Jerusalem in AD 70?

_____

_____

_____

_____

_____

The elect (13:20). In the New Testament the "elect" refers not to Israel as a nation, but to all true believers in Christ. See verse 27.

7. a. What appears to be the greatest single temptation that will face Christians during the "days of distress" (13:22-23)?

_____

_____

   b. What do Christ's words "if that were possible" (13:22) mean to you?

_____

_____

_____

_____

The Son of Man (13:24-27)

8. In your own words, state what sorts of events will immediately precede the second coming of Christ (13:24-25).

_____

_____

_____

9. Compare Mark 12:26 with Daniel 7:13-14. What is Jesus saying about Himself?

_____

_____

_____

_____

Be alert! (13:28-37)

This generation (13:30). This may be the single most difficult phrase in all of Mark's Gospel. If "all these things" (v. 30) refers to events that include the second coming of Christ, then Jesus was saying that He would come within the lifetime of some of His disciples—and was therefore mistaken. Some interpreters try to overcome this difficulty by saying that "generation" refers to something besides a period of thirty years or so. From a strictly semantic viewpoint, however, this is highly unlikely.

A more promising alternative is to note that the phrase "these things" also occurs in the immediately preceding verse (13:29), where it refers to events leading up to, but not including, the second coming of Christ. In this case Jesus is not saying that the "distress" He foretells will end within the lifetime of His disciples, but that "these things"— calamities leading up to but not including His second coming—must happen within that time. At the same time, Jesus is not ruling out further distress, nor is He saying that He will return within the lifetime of His disciples.

For Thought and Discussion: Which events described by Jesus in Mark 13 have already occurred? Which are still to come?

For Thought and Discussion: How do you think the disciples would have responded if Jesus had told them He would not return for at least 2,000 years?

Optional Application: List specific ways in which Christians today need to "be alert" and "watch" (13:33,37), and ask God to help you obey these commands of Jesus.

What Jesus is saying, then, is not that He will return within a generation, but that He will *not* return until certain things have occurred. "These things" were most certainly fulfilled with the terrible events surrounding the fall of Jerusalem in AD 70. But "these things" were not necessarily *exhausted* by the fall of Jerusalem. Jesus is not concerned about predicting when He will return; indeed, He makes it clear that even He does not know the date of His coming (13:32). Rather, He is intent upon warning His disciples that they will have to go through very tough times before He returns (13:9-20), and that many false Christs will appear prior to His coming (13:5-6,21-23). Both of these things occurred within a generation of His words (see, for example, 2 Thessalonians 2:1-2 and 1 John 2:18).

10. Why do you think God has chosen not to reveal when Christ will return?

_____

_____

_____

11. Write down any questions you have about Mark 13.

_____

_____

_____

For the group

Warm-up. Have group members share what they had read or been taught about the second coming of Christ prior to reading Mark 13 and preparing this lesson.

Read aloud and summarize.

Questions. Point out that Jesus begins and ends this discourse with the same word: "Watch." In each instance, Jesus is alerting His disciples to different temptations (13:5-6,35-37). Have group members state in their own words the two things for which we are to "watch."

Jesus uses other words, such as "be on your guard" and "be alert," to warn the disciples. Try to identify all the warnings of Mark 13.

Take note that chapter 13 is the single longest discourse of Jesus in Mark's Gospel. Why is it so important that it requires more space than any other teaching of Jesus recorded by Mark?

Jesus speaks of those who will be persecuted for their faith (13:9-13). As Christians who, as a general rule, have not experienced such persecution, we can nevertheless minister to those who are currently suffering for Jesus' sake. Have someone from your study group write to an organization that works on behalf of Christians being persecuted for their faith in other parts of the world, asking how you can help support fellow Christians being persecuted for their faith. (If no one knows of such an organization, suggest the Christian Rescue Effort for the Emancipation of Dissidents [CREED], 787 Princeton Kingston Rd., Princeton, NJ 08540.)

Jesus also spoke about preaching the gospel to "all nations" (see note above on 13:13). Almost three billion people from some 17,000 distinct people-groups have still not heard the gospel of Christ. An organization committed to reaching these people is Frontier Fellowship, Inc., Pasadena, CA 91104. Write them and ask how you can help reach the world for Christ. Or, write to The Navigators (International Ministries Department, P.O. Box 6000, Colorado Springs, CO 80934).

Summarize.

Wrap-up. Encourage group members to spend time this coming week reflecting on what practical effect the promises and warnings of Jesus in Mark 13 should have on their lives.

Worship. Thank God for the assurance that Christ is returning, and that His words, unlike the things of this world, will never pass away (13:31).

1. D. A. Carson, *Matthew* in *The Expositor's Bible Commentary*, Volume 8 (Grand Rapids, MI: Zondervan, 1984), page 498.
2. Carson, *Matthew*, page 501.

MARK 14:1-42

Countdown to Betrayal

Jesus had foretold the future (Mark 13). Now it was time to come back to the present realities of His impending death and resurrection. For it was precisely Jesus' sufferings on the cross that would open the way for His glorious return at the end of the age.

"Not during the feast" (14:1-2)

Passover (14:1). The Jewish festival commemorating the night when the angel of the Lord "passed over" the homes of the Israelites dwelling in Egypt and killed all the firstborn sons of the Egyptians (see Exodus 12:1-30). In first-century Jerusalem the lambs used in the feast were killed on the fourteenth of Nisan (March/April). The meal was then eaten that evening after sundown, which by Jewish reckoning would be the fifteenth of Nisan, since the Jewish day began at sundown.

Feast of Unleavened Bread (14:1). This feast followed Passover and lasted seven days. Jewish pilgrims from all over the Roman Empire came to Jerusalem to celebrate Passover and the Feast of Unleavened Bread.

1. Why did the Jewish leaders not wish to arrest Jesus during the Feast of Unleavened Bread (14:2)? What

133

Optional Application:
How is this woman's act
of worship an example
for us in our worship?

does this indicate about the attitude of many of the
common people toward Jesus?

_____

_____

_____

Anointing for burial (14:3-9)

Simon the Leper (14:3). Probably a man whom Jesus
had healed of leprosy.

A woman (14:3). If this is a parallel account of John
12:1-8, which is likely, the woman was Mary, sister
of Martha and Lazarus, the man whom Jesus
raised from the dead (John 11). Although Luke
7:36-50 is similar to Mark 14:3-9 and John 12:1-8,
the differences are such that Luke must be record-
ing a different incident.

Some of those present (14:4). Matthew 26:8 tells us
that it was Jesus' disciples who were indignant.

A year's wages (14:5). Literally, "three hundred
denarii." See note on Mark 6:37.

The poor (14:5). "The mention of the poor is natural
because it was the custom for the Jews to give
gifts to the poor on the evening of the Passover."[1]

2. How would *you* have felt had you witnessed this
woman pouring out a full year's wages worth of
perfume on someone's head (14:3-5)?

_____

_____

_____

_____

3. What does this incident tell you about the disciples'
level of understanding of who Jesus was and why
He came?

_____

_____

_____

_____

4. Old Testament prophets often acted out the events they were predicting (see, for instance, Jeremiah 27:1-15, 28:10-11). Do you think this woman knew she was acting out a prophecy of Jesus' death (Mark 14:8)? Why or why not?

_____

_____

_____

_____

For Further Study:
Compare the four Gospel accounts of Judas. Then do the following:
  a. Make a list of factors you see— whether in Judas's personality, beliefs or circumstances—which might have contributed toward his betraying Jesus.
  b. Then consider your list and ponder whether any of these factors might be potential stumbling blocks in your own life.

Judas sells out (14:10-11)

_____

Judas Iscariot (14:10). Matthew's Gospel (26:15) tells us Judas received thirty pieces of silver (a rather paltry amount) for betraying Jesus, while John's Gospel (12:6, 13:29) notes that he was the one who carried the money bag for the Twelve.

_____

5. Neither Mark nor any of the other Gospel writers tells us just why Judas betrayed Jesus. What do you think might have motivated Judas to do this? (Nobody knows the "right" answer, but try to reason out some possibilities.)

_____

_____

_____

_____

For Further Study:
Read carefully Hebrews
8:1–10:18, and compare the Old Covenant
God made with Israel
with the New Covenant
God made through the
blood of Jesus.

The Last Supper (14:12-26)

First day of the Feast (14:12). The following phrase, "when it was customary to sacrifice the Passover Lamb," makes it clear that Mark is talking about Nisan 14, or the day of Passover itself, and not the day following. The Last Supper was therefore a Passover meal.

A man carrying a jar of water (14:13). Such a sight would be unusual, since women normally carried the water jars.

A large upper room, furnished and ready (14:15). As with His triumphal entry into Jerusalem, Jesus had made advance preparations for this event. This indicates that He had a circle of disciples in the Jerusalem area in addition to the Twelve.

6. On the Passover day itself, the disciples of Jesus had no idea of where they would celebrate the meal! Why did Jesus arrange for the Passover meal in such a secretive manner (14:12-15)?

_____

_____

_____

_____

Just as it is written (14:21). Jesus was probably referring to Isaiah 53, the famous "suffering servant" prophecy. This Old Testament passage was quoted frequently by the first Christians immediately following Jesus' ascension, and Isaiah's title "servant of the Lord" was one of the earliest messianic titles for Jesus (see Acts 3:13,26; 4:27,30; 8:32-35).

7. Judas was held accountable for Jesus' death even though Jesus Himself declared it was foreordained that He should die this way (14:21). What does this say about God's sovereignty and man's moral accountability?

_____

_____

_____

_____

For Thought and Discussion: Discuss your response to question 7 in light of 1 Corinthians 5:7.

Jesus took bread (14:22). Unleavened bread, or matzoth, was eaten at Passover together with the roasted lamb, bitter herbs, and wine. Following the meal, the head of the household would break the remaining matzoth and distribute it. Mark is probably referring to this distribution, which followed the main meal itself (compare Luke 22:19-20 and 1 Corinthians 11:23-25, where the words "in the same way, after supper" may indicate that both the bread and the cup of the New Covenant were distributed following the main Passover meal).

He took the cup (14:23). Four cups of wine, symbolic of God's four promises to Israel on the first Passover (Exodus 6:6-7), were shared at different stages of the meal. The cup of which Mark speaks was the third cup, "the cup of redemption," symbolic of the promise "I will redeem you with an outstretched arm."

Blood of the covenant (14:24). The Old Covenant was made possible by the blood of the Passover Lamb, which freed the people of Israel from bondage in Egypt. Forgiveness of sins under the Old Covenant also required blood sacrifice (see Leviticus 16 for a description of *Yom Kippur*, the Day of Atonement). As another New Testament writer put it, "without the shedding of blood there is no forgiveness" (Hebrews 9:22), and therefore no possibility of a covenant between God and humankind.

For Thought and Discussion: What would have happened to the ancient Israelites had they not painted the blood of the Passover lamb on their doorposts (see Exodus 12:13, 22-23)? What will happen to us if the "doorposts" of our lives are not covered with the blood of the new Passover lamb, Jesus Christ?

Optional Application: Arrange to celebrate the Lord's Supper as a group. Afterward, talk about what that experience means to you in light of Mark 14.

8. a. At the traditional Passover celebration the central emphasis was on the sacrifical lamb, the main course. Where did Jesus place His emphasis (14:22-24)?

_____

b. Why did He do this?

_____

Optional Application:
Can you identify with
Peter in Mark 14:30-31?
Have you ever been that
sure of yourself? What
should we learn from
Peter's example?

**For Thought and
Discussion:** What new
truths about the human-
ity of Jesus did you learn
from this lesson?

9. What promise was Jesus making to His disciples in
Mark 14:25?

_____

_____

_____

_____

A hymn (14:26). The Passover celebration ended with
the people singing the second part of the Hallel,
Psalms 115:18.

"You will all fall away" (14:27-31)

10. How did Jesus give a word of hope to His followers
even as He foretold their failure (14:27-28)?

_____

_____

_____

11. What do you think motivated Peter to insist that he
would not disown Jesus (14:29,31)?

_____

_____

_____

Gethsemane (14:32-42)

Abba (14:36). An Aramaic intimate form for father
("Daddy"). The Jews did not use this word to
address God, thinking it too familiar and therefore
disrespectful. Jesus not only used it Himself, but

encouraged His disciples to do so (see Matthew 6:9 and Romans 8:15).

12. a. Read carefully Mark 14:36. Did God grant Jesus' request?

_____

b. What does this teach you about prayer?

_____

_____

_____

Body (14:38). Mark doesn't use the Greek word that normally designates the human body, but rather the word normally translated "flesh." Paul often uses "flesh" as a theological term to designate sinful human nature (in Romans 7:5,25, NIV translates "flesh" as "sinful nature"), but here "flesh" is more likely meant to emphasize human weakness than human sin. The notion of the human body *per se* being sinful is foreign to biblical thought; Greeks believed matter was evil, but Hebrews did not. And while it is true that the disciples were suffering from bodily fatigue, Jesus pinpoints their real problem as a lack of prayer.

13. If Mark's readers were indeed Roman Christians undergoing persecution, how would this section of his Gospel apply to them?

_____

_____

_____

_____

14. List any questions you have about this section.

_____

_____

_____

139

For the group

Warm-up. What would you think if you were attending a dinner party for a prominent Christian leader, and a woman made a scene kissing his feet while he praised her for doing so?

Read aloud and summarize.

Questions. Draw attention to Mark's statement that the final week of Jesus' earthly ministry was Passover week. Make sure your discussion brings out the significance of this.

Compare Peter's promise to persevere (14:29,31) with his lack of persevering prayer in Gethsemane (14:37-41). How can we overcome such disparities between what we profess and what we do?

Mark 14:13,17,25,28,42 all indicate that Jesus was in complete control of the events of that final week. What significance does this have for your faith in Christ?

Summarize.

Wrap-up.

Worship.

1. Wessel, *Mark*, page 756.

MARK 14:43–15:15

Arrest and Trial

The hour had come (Mark 14:42). The powers of darkness—the religious leaders of Jerusalem!—unleashed their wrath against Jesus. In one sense, they understood His message of the Kingdom better than did the disciples. They knew it spelled the end to religion as they practiced it!

Jesus' trial, held in the shadows of night and early morning, was a battle whose outcome was decided even before it began. Jesus did not resist that outcome but spoke only when He needed to declare the truth about Himself and His mission. Indeed, only He acted truthfully throughout the night before His death. The religious leaders, Pilate, and even His disciples all succumbed to the lie that Jesus' death would put an end to this whole business of His being the "Messiah."

Jesus betrayed and arrested (14:43-52)

A crowd armed with swords and clubs (14:43). Luke 22:52 mentions "officers of the temple guards" as being among the crowd, while John 18:3 refers to "soldiers." The officers would be Jews, the soldiers almost certainly Romans. All four Gospels agree that the Jewish religious leaders were the driving force behind the arrest and execution of Jesus.

One of those standing near (14:47). John 18:10 tells us it was Peter.

1. Why did the religious leaders bring a large, armed crowd to arrest Jesus (14:43,48)? What does this tell you about their understanding of what Jesus was trying to do?

_____

_____

_____

_____

2. Peter tried to attack one of the mob. What does this act tell you about Peter?

_____

_____

_____

_____

3. a. Only minutes (maybe an hour or two) earlier, Jesus was "overwhelmed with sorrow to the point of death" (14:34). How do you read His emotions during the arrest?

_____

_____

_____

b. Why do you think Jesus was able to handle the moment of crisis with courage, while His followers were not?

_____

_____

_____

_____

A young man (14:51). Many commentators believe the traditional author of this Gospel, John Mark, here refers to himself. The question then arises, why would Mark have been with Jesus and the disciples at Gethsemane? A possible answer is that Jesus and the Twelve ate the Last Supper at the house of John Mark. The following facts, though not conclusive, are consistent with this hypothesis:

1. Mary, the mother of John Mark, opened her home to meetings of the early Jerusalem Church, even when the Church was being persecuted. "Many people" were able to gather there (Acts 12:12), indicating that the house was large, and that the family was therefore at least fairly well-to-do.

In line with this, we note that the Last Supper took place in "a large upper room," probably indicating a house with more than one such room, and therefore the house of a family of means. Also, the young man of Mark 14:51 wore an outer garment made not of wool, as were most such garments, but of linen, an expensive material worn only by the wealthy.

2. The Apostle Peter was so well known to the family that Mary's servant, Rhoda, recognized his voice (Acts 12:14). And in 1 Peter 5:13 the apostle calls Mark "my son." As stated previously, tradition holds that Mark wrote this Gospel based upon the preaching of Peter.

The fact that John Mark was a native of Jerusalem and knew Peter well makes it eminently reasonable (though not an established fact) that Mark and his family were part of the Jerusalem circle of disciples who believed in Jesus during His earthly ministry. Furthermore, the incident recorded in 14:51-52 is totally irrelevant to the flow of Mark's narrative—unless the author is saying, "I was there!"

But how could John Mark have been there? As a curious young lad well-acquainted with Jesus and Peter, he may have slipped out of bed (thus wearing only an outer garment as a nightshirt) and followed Jesus and the disciples when they left his house for Gethsemane late that night following the Last Supper. If this is the case, then the events recorded in this Gospel account surrounding the last week of Jesus' earthly ministry have an eyewitness quality that goes beyond the preaching of Peter to the writer himself.[1]

The trial of Jesus (14:53-65)

Sanhedrin (14:55). The high court of Judaism, composed of the chief priests and other prominent religious leaders of Jerusalem. If all the members were present, there would have been seventy of them. (See also Acts 4:5-22 and 23:1-10.)

This nighttime gathering of the Sanhedrin was highly unusual and perhaps illegal. At the same time, we must keep in mind that certain "loopholes" may have existed in Sanhedrin procedures which would permit this sort of speedy nocturnal trial under extreme circumstances. As Jesus Himself noted, the Pharisees and teachers of the law were famous for creating exceptions to established rules in order to justify their deeds (Mark 7:9-13). So most, if not all, of the procedures at the trial of Jesus may have been legal, if not usual.[2]

Be that as it may, Mark's account portrays the trial of Jesus as a sort of "kangaroo court," with a parade of prearranged false witnesses and no real opportunity for a defense on Jesus' part. Whether or not strictly legal, it was certainly not fair.

4. Why did the Sanhedrin have such a hard time convicting Jesus of any crime (14:55-59)?

_____

_____

_____

_____

5. Why do you think Jesus did not answer the charges brought against Him (14:61)?

_____

_____

_____

_____

The high priest asked him (14:61). If William Barclay is correct, the high priest's question was illegal, since he asked Jesus to testify against Himself.[3] D. A. Carson, on the other hand, notes that according to Matthew's account, the high priest placed Jesus under a binding legal oath, thus compelling Him to answer.[4] The fact that Mark mentions no oath, however, indicates that Jesus answered because He chose to do so. Compare Jesus' reply with Psalm 110:1 and Daniel 7:14.

6. Why do you think Jesus chose to answer the high priest's question (14:61-62) after refusing to respond to the false charges brought against Him?

_____

_____

_____

_____

7. What was Jesus claiming about Himself in 14:62?

_____

_____

_____

_____

Tore his clothes (14:63). The tearing of one's clothes was originally a sign of great grief (see Genesis 37:29 and 2 Kings 18:37). In the case of the high priest, it became "a formal judicial act" in response to blasphemy, "minutely regulated by the Talmud."[5] See also the note on Mark 2:7 ("Blaspheming") in lesson 3 (page 32).

Worthy of death (14:64). Leviticus 24:14 mandates death by stoning as the penalty for blasphemy.

Peter's threefold denial (14:66-72)

8. What do you learn about Peter from his presence in the courtyard outside where Jesus was being tried and from his subsequent behavior?

145

Have you ever done something you thought God could not forgive? Consider Peter's three-fold denial of Jesus (14:66-72), and thank God that Christ forgave even this most terrible of sins.

Optional Application: How do other people's attitudes toward Jesus Christ affect your willingness to talk about your Christian faith? Pray for strength to affirm your faith in Christ in situations where others may be indifferent or hostile to Him.

9. How does reading about Peter's denial make you feel? Why?

_____

_____

_____

You are a Galilean (14:70). Galilean Jews looked no different from their Jerusalem counterparts, but did speak with a distinctive accent (see Matthew 26:73).

Jesus before Pilate (15:1-15)

Pilate (15:1). Pontius Pilate was the Roman governor of Judea from AD 26 to 36. According to the Jewish historian Josephus, he did not hesitate to quell local insurrections with brutal dispatch. Jesus Himself called attention to Pilate's repression on at least one occasion (Luke 13:1). On the other hand, Pilate was no mere despot, but acted according to Roman civil law when investigating cases brought before him. In the final analysis, he owed his position to the pleasure of the Roman emperor and was for this reason more motivated to placate the local populace than to administer exact justice.[6]

The Jews brought Jesus to Pilate because under the Roman occupation they could not legally put someone to death (John 18:31), except in cases where the sanctity of the Temple had been violated (see, for example, Acts 7:59 and 21:27-32).[7]

King of the Jews (15:2). When Jesus acknowledged the title "Son of David" (Mark 10:47-48) and rode into Jerusalem in fulfillment of Zechariah 9:9 (Mark 11:1-11), He was in fact proclaiming Himself "King of the Jews." The Jews brought this charge not for religious reasons, however, but for political reasons, hoping Pilate would condemn Jesus as one who desired to usurp the authority of the Roman emperor.

---

10. Contrast the way Jesus responded to the Sanhedrin and to Pilate with the way Peter responded to those who questioned him.

_____

_____

_____

_____

Insurrectionists (15:7). Probably Zealots (see note on Mark 3:18, lesson 4, pages 42-43). "The uprising" to which Mark refers could have been any one of many local outbreaks of violence instigated by the Zealots.

11. The crowd probably came to Pilate to ask for the release of Barabbas (15:6-8).

a. Why did Pilate try to "change the subject" and try to have Jesus released instead (15:9)?

_____

_____

_____

_____

b. Why did he finally capitulate to the crowd (15:15)?

_____

_____

_____

_____

For Further Study:
In the providence of God, Jesus was executed by crucifixion (a Roman form of capital punishment) rather than being stoned (the usual way in which Jews executed blasphemers). Read Deuteronomy 21:22-23, Galatians 3:13-14, and 2 Corinthians 5:21. Why did Jesus have to be crucified, not stoned, in order to accomplish His mission of "giving his life as a ransom for many" (Mark 10:45)?

Optional Application:
Pilate did something he really did not want to do. Have you ever felt that way? What did you do? If you are presently undergoing such a temptation, ask God for strength and wisdom to respond as you should.

Optional Application:
Have you ever been
betrayed or abandoned
by a friend? How did it
feel? Does it make any
difference to you that
Jesus knows what that
feels like? Why?

Flogged (15:15). This was no mere punitive beating.
The whip used in flogging a prisoner consisted of
several pieces of leather, onto which were tied
pieces of metal and bone. The Jews mercifully limited flogging to a maximum of forty stripes; the
Romans had no such limitation. In many cases
the victims of Roman floggings did not survive.
According to John 19:1-5, Pilate apparently had
Jesus flogged in a last-ditch attempt to elicit mercy
from the crowd so that they would consent to his
freeing Jesus.

12. What do you learn about Jesus from the way He
handled His arrest and trial?

_____

_____

_____

_____

_____

13. Write down any further questions you have about
the events surrounding the arrest and trial of Jesus.

_____

_____

_____

_____

_____

For the group

Warm-up. Ask group members what sorts of situations
make them feel uncomfortable or fearful about sharing
their faith.

Read aloud and summarize.

Questions. Try to get group members to empathize
with all of the people involved in the arrest and trial of

Jesus (Peter, the other disciples, the soldiers, Judas, the Jewish leaders, the crowd, Pilate). Talk about their hopes, fears, strengths, and weaknesses. Try to figure out their motives for doing what they did. Ask group members whom they can identify with most easily and least easily.

Talk about what these scenes reveal about Jesus. What picture do you get of Him? Is He someone you can respect? Why?

Summarize.

Wrap-up. Encourage people to reflect on how their lives would be different if Jesus, like Peter and the rest of the disciples, had chosen to take the easy way out and refused to tell the Sanhedrin and Pilate just who He was (and is!).

Worship. Thank God for His faithfulness to His promises, as exemplified by Christ's perseverance in going to the cross.

1. For an alternative theory, see Barclay, *The Gospel of Mark*, pages 365-366.
2. See Carson, *Matthew*, pages 549-552, for a survey of recent studies on the trial of Jesus.
3. Barclay, *The Gospel of Mark*, pages 368-9.
4. Carson, *Matthew*, page 554.
5. Vincent Taylor, *The Gospel According to St. Mark* (London: Macmillan, 1952), page 569.
6. See the article "Pilate, Pontius" in *The International Standard Bible Encyclopedia*, Revised Edition, Volume Three (Grand Rapids, MI: Eerdmans, 1986), pages 867-869.
7. F. F. Bruce, *The Book of Acts* (Grand Rapids, MI: Eerdmans, 1954), pages 169-170, 433-434.

MARK 15:16-47

The Death of the Messiah

It was the darkest hour in the history of God's people. The religious leaders of Israel had condemned their Messiah to death, and the worldly rulers of Rome were carrying out the sentence. Even the skies above Jerusalem fell under darkness, though it was the middle of the day (15:33).

The fact that Jesus was crucified was final proof to many that He could not be the Messiah. Did not God's own Law say that anyone hung upon a tree was under God's curse (Deuteronomy 21:23)? How could the Messiah be the cursed one?

Yet even as Jesus died, God gave the high priests of the temple a clue as to what this Man's death had accomplished: the curtain separating the Holy Place from the Holy of Holies was torn in two (Mark 15:38). Only later would the meaning of this event become clear.

Via Dolorosa (Path of Sorrows) (15:16-23)

Soldiers (15:16). These Roman soldiers were probably among those who had accompanied Pilate from Caesarea (the headquarters of the procurator of Palestine) to Jerusalem. Their presence in Jerusalem, as well as that of Pilate, was no doubt meant to ensure that the potential instability created by the masses of Jewish pilgrims during Passover remained just that—potential, and nothing more.

For Thought and Discussion: a. How is what the soldiers did to Jesus a picture of the way humans typically respond to God?

b. How does God respond when humans treat Him like this? What does this tell you about God?

Optional Application: Have you ever been ridiculed for being a Christian? How did it make you feel? How did you respond?

"Hail, king of the Jews!" (15:18). This mockery was most likely a parody of the Roman "Hail, Emperor Caesar!"[1]

1. How did the Roman soldiers attack Jesus . . .

physically? _____

_____

_____

emotionally? _____

_____

_____

2. Why didn't Jesus strike them dead for doing this?

_____

_____

_____

Simon . . . carry the cross (15:21). Simon was from Cyrene, capital city of Rome's North African province of Cyrenaica (Libya). It contained a large colony of Jews.[2] Since Simon is a common Jewish name, this man was either a pilgrim in Jerusalem for Passover, or a Jewish native of Cyrene who had moved to Jerusalem (Acts 6:9 mentions a synagogue "of the Cyrenians" in Jerusalem, indicating that not a few of Simon's countrymen had moved to the Holy City). Mark probably mentions Simon's two sons because they were known to the Roman church (note Paul's mention of a man named Rufus in Romans 16:13).

The "cross" Simon was forced to carry was the heavy wooden crosspiece on which the victim was to be nailed. This crosspiece usually weighed thirty to forty pounds and was strapped to the victim's shoulders.[3] Jesus was apparently so weakened by the flogging He had received (not to mention the crown of thorns!) that the soldiers had to press Simon into service.

3. Simon's encounter with Christ was most unusual. How did you first "encounter Christ"?

_____

_____

_____

_____

Wine mixed with myrrh (15:23). Such a mixture was used as a narcotic, to help lessen the victim's pain. Since consideration of the victim seems out of character for Roman soldiers as Mark depicts them, perhaps local Jews prepared the mixture whenever Rome crucified one of their people.

4. Why do you think Jesus refused the wine mixed with myrrh?

_____

_____

_____

_____

The crucified king (15:24-32)

And they crucified him (15:24). Mark shows remarkable restraint in recounting what Cicero called "the cruelest and most hideous punishment possible."[4] Jesus, already half-dead from a flogging, was now stripped of His blood-clotted clothing and laid upon the ground, His arms spread atop the crosspiece. A soldier then drove a large iron nail through each of Jesus' wrists into the crosspiece. The crosspiece was then hoisted into place atop a vertical beam already placed in the ground. Finally, Jesus' legs were either nailed or tied to the vertical beam (John 20:25 mentions nail holes in Jesus' hands only). A slow, agonizing death now awaited Him.

The third hour (15:25). Around nine o'clock in the morning by both Jewish and Roman reckoning.

For Thought and Discussion: What is the significance of the fact that David wrote Psalm 22 hundreds of years before the Jews knew anything about crucifixion (a Roman form of execution)?

For Thought and Discussion: How would your life be different if Jesus had taken up the religious leaders' challenge and come down off the cross?

Neither Matthew nor Luke, who otherwise follows Mark's chronology, includes this statement. John 19:14 places the crucifixion sometime after "the sixth hour." Many solutions have been proposed for this difference.

Perhaps B. F. Westcott's explanation, that John was using a system of reckoning time familiar to his readers in Asia Minor (Ephesus?), is still as plausible as any. In that case, John 19:14 would have Jesus still with Pilate at about six a.m. (the "sixth hour" by John's reckoning), rather than at noon.[5] This not only makes John's narrative consistent with Mark's, but also avoids the problem of how Jesus could have gone from Pilate's presence on a long procession through the streets of Jerusalem to Golgotha, been crucified, died, and been prepared for burial, all between noon and sunset (which would still be relatively early at Passover time).

The written notice (15:26). All criminals sentenced to death by crucifixion were paraded through the streets of the city with a written notice proclaiming their crime in large letters. Once outside the city at the site of the execution, the soldiers attached the notice to the victim's cross. The notice served as a warning to any who would repeat the crime.

Two robbers (15:27). The Greek word literally means "insurrectionists." So far as Rome was concerned, Jesus was attempting to make Himself a king and thereby displace the authority of Caesar. Thus they crucified Him between two men (probably Zealots) who sought to overthrow Roman rule in Judea.

5. Read Mark 15:24 in light of Psalm 22:18. Then read all of Psalm 22 and write down every allusion to this psalm (explicit or implied) in Mark's account of the crucifixion.

_____

_____

_____

_____

For Thought and
Discussion: Pause to
contemplate the suffer-
ings Jesus went through
prior to His death, and
write down your feelings.

6. Why did Jesus not take up the religious leaders'
challenge and rescue Himself, thus proving His
messiahship (15:32)?

_____

_____

_____

_____

7. Jesus was crucified between, and thus identified
with, two criminals. What significance does this
have for your life?

_____

_____

_____

_____

Darkness at noon (15:33-36)

At the sixth hour . . . until the ninth hour (15:33).
Between noon and three p.m.

He's calling Elijah (15:35). Jews regarded Elijah as a
deliverer of those in trouble.[6] The people either
misunderstood Jesus' call of "My God" (Hebrew
Eli; Aramaic *Eloi*) as referring to Elijah, or were
being sarcastic.

8. Why do you think Jesus quoted Psalm 22:1 for all
to hear (15:34)?

_____

_____

_____

_____

155

Optional Application:
Read Mark 15:38 and
Hebrews 10:19-25.
What difference does it
make to you personally
that the curtain that
screened the Most Holy
Place was torn when
Jesus died?

The death that leads to life (15:37-41)

9. Jesus cried out in a loud voice twice (15:34,37) just
before He died.

a. What does this indicate about the amount of
strength He had left?

_____

_____

_____

b. What does this tell you about the way He died?

_____

_____

_____

The curtain of the temple (15:38). The Old Testament
tabernacle, which symbolized God's dwelling place
with Israel, had two principal areas: the "Holy
Place" and the "Most Holy Place." There were thus
curtains, one separating the "Holy Place" from the
"Most Holy Place," and the other separating both
from the outer area (Exodus 26:30-37; see also
Hebrews 9:2-4).

The priests entered the Holy Place daily to
offer incense and bread, but the Most Holy Place
was reserved for one yearly sacrifice only: that of
Yom Kippur, the Day of Atonement. On that day
the high priest entered the Most Holy Place with
the blood of the animal sacrificed for the sins of all
Israel. He sprinkled this blood on the Ark of the
Covenant as an atonement for the sins of all the
people. Only the high priest could do this, and only
once a year (see Leviticus 16:17 and Hebrews 9:7).

When Israel built the Temple to replace the
tabernacle, the same pattern was followed. Thus in
Jesus' day there were two curtains in the temple.
Mark is almost certainly referring to the inner curtain, which separated the Holy Place from the
Most Holy Place. This curtain was made of very
heavy material, tightly woven and virtually impossible to tear. The fact that it was torn from top to

bottom suggests the imagery of an invisible sword cutting it in two. Mark is clearly talking about a supernatural event.

_____

10. What do you think the tearing of the Temple curtain symbolized?

_____

_____

_____

_____

11. a. The centurion believed in Jesus because of "how He died" (15:39). What do you think Mark meant by this statement?

_____

_____

_____

_____

b. What is there about how Jesus died that we might apply to how we should *live*?

_____

_____

_____

_____

For Thought and Discussion: In Mark 15:39 a Roman soldier recognizes the great truth that the religious leaders could not see. Discuss the significance of this for Mark's readers, and for yourself.

Jesus is buried (15:42-47)

Joseph of Arimathea (15:43). Mark called Joseph a "prominent member of the Council," i.e., the Sanhedrin. The word translated "prominent" by the NIV may also be rendered "of good repute," referring not to Joseph's rank in the Sanhedrin, but rather to his reputation as a just man. Luke has evidently interpreted it in this way, adding that Joseph did not consent to the Sanhedrin's condemnation of Jesus (Luke 23:50-51). Joseph was "awaiting the Kingdom of God" of which Jesus spoke, though John 19:38 tells us he kept his allegiance to Jesus secret for fear of the Jewish authorities. Matthew notes that Joseph was wealthy, perhaps because Matthew was emphasizing the fulfillment of prophecy (see Isaiah 53:9).

Arimathea was probably the same village where the prophet Samuel was born (Ramathaim; see 1 Samuel 1:1), located about twenty miles north of Jerusalem.

12. Mark emphasizes that Joseph showed courage in asking for Jesus' body (15:43). What risks was Joseph taking in approaching Pilate with this request?

_____

_____

_____

_____

_____

13. How do you feel after studying the account of Jesus' death?

_____

_____

_____

_____

14. List any questions you have about this section.

_____

_____

_____

_____

For the group

Warm-up. When you see a cross in or on a church building, what does it mean to you?

Read aloud and summarize.

Questions. Try to help group members feel the intensity of the events recorded in Mark 15:16-47. Read and discuss this passage with your emotions as well as with your intellect.
Draw attention to Mark 15:38. This is the first thing Mark mentions after Jesus' death. Ask group members why they think Mark mentioned this before all else. Then ask them why the Roman centurion's confession is the very next event recorded by Mark.
Joseph of Arimathea was part of the "religious establishment" that condemned Jesus, yet he himself did not approve. Discuss this fact in light of our tendency to categorize people by their class or status.

Summarize.

Wrap-up. Have people share what the death of Jesus means to them personally. Encourage them to reflect upon both this week's lesson—the death of Christ—and next week's lesson—the resurrection.

Worship. Thank God for what Christ's death has accomplished for sinful people. Sing a hymn which focuses on this subject.

1. Wessel, *Mark*, page 777.
2. "Cyrene" in *The International Standard Bible Encyclopedia,* Volume One (Revised Edition), pages 844-845.
3. Wessel, *Mark*, page 778.
4. Cicero, *In Verram*, 5.64.165.
5. B. F. Westcott, *The Gospel According to St. John* (Grand Rapids, MI: Eerdmans, 1967; reprint of 1881 edition), page 282.
6. Wessel, *Mark*, page 782.

MARK 16:1-20

"He Is Risen!"

Jesus' death had scattered His disciples like frightened sheep. Only a handful of Galilean women, who had ministered to His needs during His ministry (15:41), remained to take care of His body.

Their devotion to Jesus was so strong that on the day following the Sabbath they went to the tomb to anoint His body as a token of their love for Him. Not until they neared the tomb did they think about the fact that the stone covering the entrance to the tomb was too large for them to move! How then, could they anoint the body?

The answer was not long in coming: there was no body to anoint! Jesus' promise to rise again had come to pass! He had conquered the grave; death had been swallowed up in victory. The women, confused and frightened, could not take it all in at once. But their lives—and the history of all humanity—would never be the same. Read 16:1-20.

The empty tomb (16:1-8)

Anoint Jesus' body (16:1). The women were unable to anoint Jesus' body on the day of His death because He was buried shortly before sundown on Friday, the beginning of the Sabbath, and they still had to buy and prepare the spices (see Luke 23:56). They sought to anoint Jesus not for the purpose of preserving His body (the Jews did not practice embalming), but most likely to reduce the stench

161

of decomposition. (In Palestine's hot climate, bodies decomposed quickly; see, e.g., John 11:39).[1] The women's act, while largely impractical, was a gesture of love (compare Mark 14:3-9).

1. Contrast the disciples' actions (14:50) with those of these women. Write down your observations, including the feelings and possible motivations of all involved.

_____

_____

_____

_____

_____

Young man dressed in a white robe (16:5). Although Mark does not say so specifically, the young man's dress suggests that he was an angel. Compare Matthew 28:2-3.

2. Describe what you would have thought and felt had you entered the tomb with the three women (16:5).

_____

_____

_____

_____

3. Why do you think the angel instructed the women to tell his message to "the disciples *and Peter*" (16:7)?

_____

_____

_____

_____

How Did Mark End His Gospel?

The earliest and best manuscripts of Mark's Gospel end at 16:8. On the other hand, the majority of manuscripts include Mark 16:9-20 (though some do so with an asterisk, to indicate it is spurious). In addition, a number of manuscripts include a shorter ending in between verses 8 and 9, which reads as follows:

"But they reported briefly to Peter and those with him all that they had been told. And after this Jesus Himself sent out by means of them, from east to west, the sacred and imperishable proclamation of eternal salvation."

On the basis of both *external* evidence (which asks, What do the earliest and best manuscripts say?) and *internal* evidence (which asks, How do the language and style of Mark 16:9-20 compare with the rest of Mark's Gospel?), scholars are in virtually unanimous agreement that Mark did not write either verses 9-20 or the so-called "shorter ending." At the same time, verses 9-20 contain material that clearly draws on the apostolic tradition (compare, for example, Mark 16:9 with Luke 8:2, Mark 16:11 with Luke 24:11, and Mark 16:12-13 with Luke 24:13-35).

We can only speculate as to why our earliest and best copies of Mark's Gospel end at 16:8. Some believe this sudden, cryptic ending was intentional—perhaps Mark's way of saying in effect, "Even as the messiahship of Jesus and His message of the Kingdom were mysteries during His ministry, even so His resurrection was incomprehensible when it finally happened." And since he was writing to Christians, perhaps Mark ended his Gospel abruptly as a sort of ironic twist, as if to say, "But *we* know what happened—don't we?!"

On the other hand, if Mark were writing to persecuted believers in Rome, why would he end his Gospel with the word "afraid"? (Great encouragement for suffering Christians!) And why no record of the fulfillment of the promise recorded in 16:7? These and other questions lead many historians to conclude that Mark did write an ending to his Gospel, but that it was lost in the early transmission of the text. The endings we now possess may therefore represent attempts by the Church (perhaps
(continued on page 164)

For Further Study:
It would be a mistake to think Jesus' death is more important for us than is His resurrection. What did His resurrection accomplish for us? See, for example, Romans 5:10, 6:1-14, 8:11; 1 Corinthians 15:12-22.

For Thought and Discussion: How has the resurrection changed (a) human history and (b) your personal history?

(continued from page 163)
from a first-century Christian's somewhat fading memory of the original ending?) to supply what was obviously lacking.[2]

Jesus appears to His followers (16:9-14)

Mary Magdalene (16:9). Although Mark has already mentioned Mary twice (15:40,47), she is described here as though she is just being introduced. This is but one indication that a different writer penned verses 9-20.

4. Why do you think Jesus appeared first to Mary Magdalene, and not to His male disciples?

_____

_____

_____

_____

5. a. How did Jesus' disciples respond each time someone told them He rose from the dead?

_____

_____

_____

b. What do you think about this? Do you think the disciples were being thick-headed, or is their response understandable? Why?

_____

_____

_____

_____

164

The Great Commission (16:15-18)

Whoever believes and is baptized (16:16). In the early church, baptism was the visible sign of one's confession of faith in Christ—a public confession that often brought ostracism, ridicule and persecution. In other words, belief in Christ and baptism were seen as inextricably linked, virtually a single act.

6. How would you relate Jesus' emphasis on public confession of faith ("believe/baptized," 16:16) with the modern notion that religion is merely a "personal matter" between God and the individual?

_____

_____

_____

_____

7. According to Jesus, what is at stake when a person responds to the gospel (16:16)? (What do you think "saved" means?)

_____

_____

_____

_____

These signs . . . (16:17-18). The first sign, casting out demons, is prominent in Mark's Gospel. In Matthew 12:28 and Luke 11:20 Jesus says this is the definitive sign that the Kingdom of God has come in His person.

The rest of the signs mentioned here are not as prominent in the New Testament. Healing by laying on of hands is mentioned in Acts 28:8 (Mark 6:13 mentions anointing the sick with oil, as does James 5:14). "Speaking in new tongues" is mentioned in Acts 2, 10 and 19 and in 1 Corinthians 12:14, while Acts 28:2-6 records an incident

For Thought and Discussion: Why is it so important to make our faith public?

For Thought and Discussion: How do Jesus' words in Mark 16:16 make you feel? Discuss your feelings as a group.

Optional Application: What do you see as your responsibility in helping to fulfill the Great Commission (Mark 16:15; see also Matthew 28:18-20)?

where Paul is bitten by a poisonous snake without ill effects. The drinking of poison without harm is not mentioned elsewhere in the New Testament.

The fact that most of these signs are mentioned outside the Gospel accounts confirms that "those who believe" in 16:17 is not limited to the eleven apostles. It should be noted, however, that not all these signs are alike. Some involve active ministry, while others are signs of God's protection from evil. The former should be sought out by the Church; the latter should be occasions of thanksgiving when they do occur, but should not be sought actively. Failure to make this distinction between ministry and God's sovereign protection has resulted in abuses such as the snake-handling cults of Appalachia.

The ascended Lord (16:19-20)

8. a. Where else does Mark mention Jesus sitting at the right hand of God?

_____

_____

   b. What, then, is the significance of the Ascension (16:19)?

_____

_____

_____

_____

9. How was the early church able to spread so rapidly (16:20)?

_____

_____

_____

10. What difference has the ascended Lord made in your life this past year?

166

_____

_____

_____

_____

11. a. How has your view of Jesus Christ changed as a
result of your study of Mark's Gospel?

_____

_____

_____

_____

_____

b. How is this affecting your life?

_____

_____

_____

_____

For the group

Warm-up. Have group members share the most extra-
ordinary event they ever witnessed or heard about.
What sort of impact did it have on you? How does that
impact compare with what you would feel if you had
been at the tomb on that first Easter morning?

Read aloud and summarize.

Questions. Again, try to get participants to feel the
impact of the Resurrection. Two thousand years later,
the resurrection of Jesus has become an article of faith
repeated Sunday after Sunday and has lost its awe-

inspiring newness for most people. Try to restore a bit of that newness.

Can you identify with the disciples' unbelief? How would you have felt upon hearing that Jesus had risen: That it was too good to be true? That such things just do not happen?

Then remind the group that on three occasions Jesus promised His disciples He would arise from the dead. Are there any promises from the Bible that you have refused to believe because they seemed too good to be true? Or did you perhaps think that such things just do not happen? Discuss this as a group.

Reflect on what you can do, as individuals and as a group, to further the Great Commission. What practical difference does it make that Jesus is now at the right hand of God, and will work with you as you seek and practice His will for your life (Mark 16:19-20)?

Summarize.

Wrap-up. Ask group members if they would like to follow their study of Mark with a break of a few weeks, followed by another book study in the LIFECHANGE series.

Worship. Thank God for all you have learned from Mark's Gospel. Pray that as a result, your life will never be the same as it was before you studied Mark.

1. Wessel, *Mark,* page 786.
2. For an in-depth discussion see Wessel, *Mark,* pages 791-793.

STUDY AIDS

For further information on the material covered in this study, consider the following sources. If your local bookstore does not have them, ask the bookstore to order them from the publisher, or find them in a seminary library. Many university and public libraries also have these books.

Historical and Background Sources

Bruce, F. F. *New Testament History* (Doubleday, 1980).
    A readable history of Herodian kings, Roman governors, philosophical schools, Jewish sects, Jesus, the early Jerusalem church, Paul, and early Gentile Christianity. Well-documented with footnotes for the serious student, but the notes do not intrude.

Harrison, E. F. *Introduction to the New Testament* (Eerdmans, 1971).
    History from Alexander the Great—who made Greek culture dominant in the biblical world—through philosophies, pagan and Jewish religions, Jesus' ministry and teaching (the weakest section), and the spread of Christianity. Very good maps and photographs of the land, art, and architecture of New Testament times.

Packer, James I., Merril C. Tenney, William White, Jr. *The Bible Almanac* (Thomas Nelson, 1980).
    One of the most accessible handbooks of the people of the Bible and how they lived. Many photos and illustrations liven an already readable text.

Concordances, Dictionaries, and Handbooks

A *concordance* lists words of the Bible alphabetically along with each verse in which the word appears. It lets you do your own word studies. An *exhaustive* concordance lists every word used in a given translation, while an *abridged* or *complete* concordance omits either some words, some occurrences of the word, or both.
    The two best exhaustive concordances are *Strong's Exhaustive Concordance* and *Young's Analytical Concordance to the Bible*. Both are available based on the

King James Version of the Bible and the New American Standard Bible. *Strong's* has an index by which you can find out which Greek or Hebrew word is used in a given English verse. *Young's* breaks up each English word it translates. However, neither concordance requires knowledge of the original language.

Among other good, less expensive concordances, *Cruden's Complete Concordance* is keyed to the King James and Revised Versions, and *The NIV Complete Concordance* is keyed to the New International Version. These include all references to every word included, but they omit "minor" words. They also lack indexes to the original languages.

A **Bible dictionary** or **Bible encyclopedia** alphabetically lists articles about people, places, doctrines, important words, customs, and geography of the Bible.

The New Bible Dictionary, edited by J. D. Douglas, F. F. Bruce, J. I. Packer, N. Hillyer, D. Guthrie, A.R. Millard, and D.J. Wiseman (Tyndale, 1982) is more comprehensive than most dictionaries. Its 1300 pages include quantities of information along with excellent maps, charts, diagrams, and an index for cross-referencing.

Unger's Bible Dictionary by Merrill F. Unger (Moody, 1979) is equally good and is available in an inexpensive paperback edition

The *Zondervan Pictorial Encyclopedia* edited by Merrill C. Tenney (Zondervan, 1975, 1976) is excellent and exhaustive, and is being revised and updated. However, its five 1000-page volumes are a financial investment, so all but very serious students may prefer to use it at a church, public, college, or seminary library.

Unlike a Bible dictionary in the above sense, *Vine's Expository Dictionary of New Testament Words* by W. E. Vine (various publishers) alphabetically lists major words used in the King James Version and defines each New Testament Greek word that KJV translates with that English word. *Vine's* lists verse references where that Greek word appears, so that you can do your own cross-references and word studies without knowing any Greek.

Vine's is a good basic book for beginners, but it is much less complete than other Greek helps for English speakers. More serious students might prefer *The New International Dictionary of New Testament Theology,* edited by Colin Brown (Zondervan), or *The Theological Dictionary of the New Testament* by Gerhard Kittel and Gerhard Friedrich, abridged in one volume by Geoffrey W. Bromiley (Eerdmans).

A **Bible atlas** can be a great aid to understanding what is going on in a book of the Bible and how geography affected events. Here is a list of a few good choices:

The Macmillan Atlas by Yohanan Aharoni and Michael Avi-Yonah (Macmillan, 1968, 1977) contains 264 maps, 89 photos, and 12 graphics. The many maps of individual events portray battles, movements of people, and changing boundaries in detail.

The New Bible Atlas by J. J. Bimson and J. P. Kane (Tyndale, 1985) has 73 maps, 34 photos, and 34 graphics. Its evangelical perspective, concise and helpful text, and excellent research make it a very useful purchase, but its greatest strength is its outstanding graphics, such as cross-sections of the Dead Sea.

The Bible Mapbook by Simon Jenkins (Lion, 1984) is much shorter and less expensive than most other atlases, so it offers a good first taste of the usefulness of maps. It contains 91 simple maps, very little text, and 20 graphics. Some of the graphics are computer-generated and intriguing.

The Moody Atlas of Bible Lands by Barry J. Beitzel (Moody, 1984) is scholarly, very evangelical, and full of theological text, indexes, and references. This admirable reference work will be too deep and costly for some, but Beitzel shows vividly how God prepared the land of Israel perfectly for the acts of salvation He was going to accomplish in it.

A **handbook** of biblical customs can also be useful. Some good ones are *Today's Handbook of Bible Times and Customs* by William L. Coleman (Bethany, 1984) and the less detailed *Daily Life in Bible Times* (Nelson, 1982).

For Small Group Leaders

The Small Group Leader's Handbook by Steve Barker et al. (InterVarsity, 1982).
Written by an InterVarsity small group with college students primarily in mind. It includes information on small group dynamics and how to lead in light of them, and many ideas for worship, building community, and outreach. It has a good chapter on doing inductive Bible study.

Getting Together: A Guide for Good Groups by Em Griffin (InterVarsity, 1982).
Applies to all kinds of groups, not just Bible studies. From his own experience, Griffin draws deep insights into why people join groups; how people relate to each other; and principles of leadership, decision making, and discussions. It is fun to read, but its 229 pages will take more time than the above book.

You Can Start a Bible Study Group by Gladys Hunt (Harold Shaw, 1984).
Builds on Hunt's thirty years of experience leading groups. This book is wonderfully focused on God's enabling. It is both clear and applicable for Bible study groups of all kinds.

How to Build a Small Groups Ministry by Neal F. McBride (NavPress, 1994).
This hands-on workbook for pastors and lay leaders includes everything you need to know to develop a plan that fits your unique church. Through basic principles, case studies, and worksheets, McBride leads you through twelve logical steps for organizing and administering a small groups ministry.

How to Lead Small Groups by Neal F. McBride (NavPress, 1990).
Covers leadership skills for all kinds of small groups—Bible study, fellowship, task, and support groups. Filled with step-by-step guidance and practical exercises to help you grasp the critical aspects of small group leadership and dynamics.

The Small Group Letter, a special section in *Discipleship Journal* (NavPress).
Unique. Its four pages per issue, six issues per year are packed with prac-

tical ideas for small groups. It stays up to date because writers discuss what they are currently doing as small group members and leaders. To subscribe, write to Subscription Services, Post Office Box 54470, Boulder, Colorado 80323-4470.

Bible Study Methods

Braga, James. *How to Study the Bible* (Multnomah, 1982).
   Clear chapters on a variety of approaches to Bible study: synthetic, geographical, cultural, historical, doctrinal, practical, and so on. Designed to help the ordinary person without seminary training to use these approaches.

Fee, Gordon, and Douglas Stuart. *How to Read the Bible For All Its Worth* (Zondervan, 1982).
   After explaining in general what interpretation (exegesis) and application (hermeneutics) are, Fee and Stuart offer chapters on interpreting and applying the different kinds of writing in the Bible: Epistles, Gospels, Old Testament Law, Old Testament narrative, the Prophets, Psalms, Wisdom, and Revelation. Fee and Stuart also suggest good commentaries on each biblical book. They write as evangelical scholars who personally recognize Scripture as God's Word for their daily lives.

Jensen, Irving L. *Independent Bible Study* (Moody, 1963), and *Enjoy Your Bible* (Moody, 1962).
   The former is a comprehensive introduction to the inductive Bible study method, especially the use of synthetic charts. The latter is a simpler introduction to the subject.

Wald, Oletta. *The Joy of Discovery in Bible Study* (Augsburg, 1975).
   Wald focuses on issues such as how to observe all that is in a text, how to ask questions of a text, how to use grammar and passage structure to see the writer's point, and so on. Very helpful on these subjects.

Titles in the LifeChange series:

WE HAVE A STUDY THAT'S RIGHT FOR YOU.

Whether you're a new believer wanting to know the basics of Christianity, a small-group leader building new groups, or someone digging deeper into God's Word, we have something for you!

From topical to inductive, NavPress studies emphasize in-depth spiritual change for believers at all levels. Each contains a combination of questions, tools, Scripture, leader's guides, and other materials for groups or individuals. If you want to study a book of the Bible, learn to handle stress, be a good parent, or communicate effectively with God, we have the resources for your Bible study needs.

Why go anywhere else?